Peonies

Gail Harland

HPS

HARDY PLANT SOCIETY

Gardening with hardy perennials

This series of booklets, produced and published by the Hardy Plant Society, covers some of the most popular garden genera, and some of the more unusual ones. Written by experts in their field, each booklet contains cultivation and propagation advice with a descriptive list of some good garden-worthy varieties, including many lesser-known ones. They may be ordered by post from:

The Hardy Plant Society at Little Orchard, Great Comberton, Nr Pershore, Worcestershire WR10 3DP or through the website at www.hardy-plant.org.uk.

Front cover: 'A bouquet of peonies'
Photographs: Gail Harland
Drawings: Sue Ward
Editor: Timothy Riggs
©Hardy Plant Society April 2013
ISBN 978-0-901687-28-9

Gardening with hardy perennials

The Hardy Plant Society

Formed in 1957 by a group of eminent gardeners and nurserymen, this international Society has a large UK and overseas membership. It provides members with information about familiar and less-well-known perennials, and their cultivation. Through conservation and publicity, the Society works towards ensuring that all garden-worthy perennial plants remain in cultivation and have the widest possible distribution.

The charitable objectives of the Society include the advancement of knowledge of hardy perennials, achieved through its website, plant displays, and publications including the members' journal, *The Hardy Plant*, the HPS Booklet Series, and leaflets. The Society also stimulates research and experiment by awarding bursaries to students and to young people in horticultural employment.

Hardy Plant Society, Little Orchard, Great Comberton, Nr Pershore, Worcestershire WR10 3DP Tel. 01386 710317
www.hardy-plant.org.uk

Contents

Gail Harland

Gail Harland was born in Aldridge in 1963 and grew up in Sutton Coldfield. She gained a BSc in Nutrition and Dietetics from The University of Wales and worked as a dietitian at The Ipswich Hospital from 1986 to 1992. She started writing articles for the horticultural press in 1993 and was awarded The Royal Horticultural Society's Diploma in Horticulture in 1999. She writes articles on gardening and avian topics, and has had work published by a number of magazines including *The Lady, Amateur Gardening, Country Smallholding* and *Parrots*. She writes a regular poultry column for the *Cage and Aviary Birds* magazine. Her books include *Photographing Your Garden*; *The Tomato Book*, written with food writer Sofia Larrinua-Craxton and published in 2009; *Grow-it Yourself, Fruit and Veg for the 'Have a go' Gardener*, published in 2010; and *Designing and Creating a Cottage Garden*, published in 2012. She supplies photographs to several picture libraries, including Garden World Images.

Gail lives in Suffolk where she has a cottage garden of about one acre, which she shares with her husband, her two sons and a variety of ducks and chickens. She is an active member of many horticultural societies, including the Royal Horticultural Society, The Alpine Garden Society, The Hardy Plant Society and The Cottage Garden Society. She was Secretary of the Peony Group of the Hardy Plant Society for ten years.

Introduction

From the turn of the year, when the bronzy-red new shoots emerge in the company of snowdrops and winter aconites, through to the interesting seed pods and coloured leaves of autumn, peonies are indispensable and delightful members of the garden team. The best-known are the flamboyant *lactiflora* cultivars, which produce extravagant and often richly fragrant flowers in early and high summer. However, there are many species of wild peonies, which have a simple elegance that many gardeners find irresistible. Also popular are the shrubby or tree peonies, providing structure, interesting foliage and dramatic flowers to the border. With a careful choice of species and cultivars it is possible to have peonies flowering in the garden from March until July.

There are peonies available for many situations in the garden, including sunny mixed borders, rock gardens and shady woodland beds, as well as a number of rarer species which require careful cultivation in the alpine house. The key to successful peony growing is to understand the conditions they require. This booklet aims to help you choose appropriate peonies for given garden situations and to cover buying, planting and caring for a selection of peonies from the hundreds of species and varieties to be found within this fascinating genus.

PEONIES IN THE WILD AND CONSERVATION ISSUES

The latest monograph on peonies, published in 2011 by Hong De-Yuan, recognises 33 species. The shrubby species, popularly known as tree peonies, are all endemic to China. They grow usually in open forests and thickets, or sometimes on grassy slopes. Species such as *Paeonia ludlowii* are used as medicinal plants Wild plants are still being dug for their root bark; this and further habitat destruction can threaten their survival. *P. qiui* has been found in only four localities and is considered to be the most endangered species in the genus.

There are two groups of herbaceous peonies (see page 12): section *Onaepia* (an anagram of *Paeonia*), with just two species, *P. brownii* and *P. californica* found in western North America, and section *Paeonia*, the largest group, with 22 species found throughout a large part of temperate Eurasia and in NW

Africa. Individual species vary greatly in their range. *P. anomala* has a very wide distribution across central Asia, whereas *P. cambessedesii*, one of the most endangered, is found only on a few sites in the Balearic Islands of Mallorca, Menorca and Cabrera. The little known species, *P. algeriensis*, is found only along the coastal mountain range of Algeria in N Africa.

Intensive land development and grazing by goats seem to be the main threats to *P. cambessedesii*, but collecting plants for medicinal use is a major threat to species survival, and not only in China. Studies by A Rocha in Bulgaria (http://www.arocha.org/int-en/work/research/plants/peonies.html) show that in the Konjavska Mountains near Sofia, *P. peregrina* is under threat because its roots are used for medicinal purposes. The reduction of traditional woodland management, allowing dense growth of shrubs and trees, is shading out the peonies in many areas. This has been a problem with the naturalised colony of *P. mascula* on Steep Holm Island in the Bristol Channel where the growth of sycamores reduced the amount of sunlight reaching the plants.

MEDICINAL AND OTHER USES

The peony takes its name from Greek mythology. In Homer's Iliad, Paeon is a healer whose herbal medicines provide instant relief. Peonies were first grown for their supposed medicinal properties. Pliny (c. 77AD) in *Historia Naturalis*, recommends the plant as a cure for stomach pains and nightmares amongst many other conditions. Gerard's Herbal, published in 1597, includes charming illustrations of the double red peony and also a double white, presumably that now sold as *P. officinalis* 'Alba Plena'. Peony seed necklaces were worn by children to ward off convulsions and indeed are sold today on internet sites promising to fight off jealousy and the evil eye.

Large quantities of both herbaceous and tree peonies are still used in Chinese traditional medicines today. They are used as antispasmodics and to treat wounds and fungal infections, and for menstrual problems. The petals of tree peonies have been shown to have high antioxidant properties.

They were used as food too. In the Middle Ages peony seeds were crushed and used as a seasoning in stews, whilst whole roots were baked and served as a side dish. Occasionally today articles promote peonies as having edible flowers, although the ones I have tried, including *P. peregrina* and the cultivar 'Sarah Bernhardt', are somewhat distasteful, but not as thoroughly disgusting as the leaves, which have a high phenol content. Jane Fearnley-Whittingstall cooked and ate a root whilst researching her book, *Peonies, The Imperial Flower*. She describes the flavour as 'reminiscent of turnips soaked in wallpaper paste mixed with turpentine'.

PEONIES IN ART AND HISTORY

Tree peonies are very popular in China, and from surviving paintings are known to have been valued as garden plants at least as far back as 400AD. They were extremely fashionable at court during the Tang Dynasty (AD618-AD907) and were grown in the imperial gardens, raised from seeds, and by grafting. In Japan they became symbolic of wealth, good fortune and masculine bravery, and featured regularly in paintings, silk panels and embroidered kimonos. They were probably first seen in England in 1787 and for many years were considered a rich man's flower, as they are slow to propagate.

In the West, Alexander Necham (born 1157), an Augustine abbot at Cirencester, wrote that 'The garden should be adorned with roses and lilies, turnsole, violets and mandrake.... And peonies'. They were known to Shakespeare, who refers to 'Thy banks with peonied and lilied brims' in *The Taming of the Shrew*. The most widely grown of the old cottage garden peonies is *Paeonia officinalis* 'Rubra Plena' of which John Parkinson wrote admiringly in 1629, 'no flower that I know so faire, great and double'. It is known as the Memorial Day Peony in the United States, where it decorated the graves of Civil War veterans.

Cultivars of *P. officinalis* became less popular after the introduction of the more flamboyant and often fragrant cultivars of the Chinese species, *P. lactiflora*. These were extremely popular during the Victorian and Edwardian eras, with huge numbers of new introductions raised in France by breeders such as Jacques Calot, Félix Crousse and Victor and Émile Lemoine. In England, James Kelway began breeding peonies in Somerset in the 1860s and his grandson, also James, took a particular interest in them and made many new introductions. During the firm's heyday, arrangements were made for trains to stop at Peony Halt, a temporary station by the nursery, to enable people to visit the displays at 'Peony Valley'.

PEONIES IN THE GARDEN

Tree peonies have been treasured for thousands of years in China. The tree peony terraces at the Summer Palace in Beijing were described by Reginald Farrer in 1914 and can still be visited today. In Japan, plants were often grown in containers, so that when in flower they could be displayed on a raised dais for ease of contemplation. In the west, *P. mascula* and *P. officinalis*, the male and female peonies (see below), and their various forms, would be important plants in the medieval monastery gardens.

Peonies are most often seen in mixed herbaceous borders with other stalwarts such as irises and delphiniums. At Giverny in France, Monet mixed them casually with irises and poppies. They fit well in relaxed cottage garden planting schemes, provided they are not crowded out by more vigorous perennials. Cultivars such as 'Duchesse de Nemours' and 'Vivid Rose' should be considered essential in a fragrant garden.

For gardening on a grand scale you could take inspiration from Penshurst Place in Kent, where they have a 100m-long border of peonies. It is planted with great restraint using just four lactiflora cultivars in shades of pink: 'Lady Alexandra Duff', 'Albert Crousse', 'Sarah Bernhardt' and 'Monsieur Jules Elie'.

Peonies can be grown in the cutting garden or on allotments, spaced 90cm apart in rows 1.2m apart, giving them plenty of space to flourish. Tree and Itoh peonies make fantastic specimen plants. Some people dislike the rather gaunt outline that some tree peonies have in winter but an under-planting of small bulbs will distract attention from the stems.

Species such as *P. mascula*, *P. peregrina* and *P. daurica* subsp. *mlokosewitschii* will grow well in light woodland situations, combining well with dicentras and hostas. Perhaps surprisingly, the single and semi-double peonies are also perfect for wildlife gardens, their pollen-rich centres being irresistibly attractive to bumblebees, which jostle with tiny solitary bees, hoverflies and skipper butterflies as they try to get prime position in the flowers. Also important is the fact that deer and rabbits do not like the taste of peonies, so, whilst gardening friends are in despair because their roses and lupins have been eaten again, you can be smugly secure in the knowledge that these herbivores will not be demolishing your favourite plants.

Botany and Classification

STRUCTURE

Peonies were once considered to be primitive plants and were included in the family *Ranunculaceae* on the basis of their simple flower, which consists of whorls of sepals, petals, stamens and carpels. However, they are now assigned to their own family, *Paeoniaceae*, and considered as a discrete group. They contain unique chemicals such as the glycoside, paeoniflorin. Josef Halda included the genus *Glaucidium* in *Paeoniaceae* but this is currently accepted to be in the *Ranunculaceae*.

Peonies are all long-lived perennials. They have buds that are enclosed by scales, large, cupped flowers, and compound leaves, usually divided into multiples of three. The number of petals is not constant within a species, but all species have numerous stamens. Most species have a variable number of carpels, but the range of carpels can be indicative of the species.

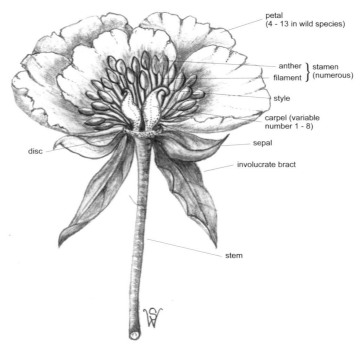

petal
(4 - 13 in wild species)

anther ⎱ stamen
filament ⎰ (numerous)

style

carpel (variable
number 1 - 8)

sepal

involucrate bract

disc

stem

Typical Peony Flower

TAXONOMY

Hong (2010) recognises three sections in the genus *Paeonia*: sect. *Moutan*, the tree peonies, and two sections of herbaceous peonies, sect. *Onaepia* and sect. *Paeonia*. In terms of growth characteristics, plants in the first section are shrubby, and although commonly known by gardeners as tree peonies, none of them is truly tree-like in form. They vary in height from low, suckering shrubs of 20cm or so to large, multi-branched specimens reaching 3.5m. The two herbaceous sections are all perennials, but vary considerably in size, root structure, leaf and flower.

section Moutan

Shrubs, all endemic to China/Tibet

> subsection *Delavayanae*
> Several flowers to stem, 1-5 carpels.
> Includes the yellow-flowered *P. ludlowii*, and the variable *P. delavayi*. (*P. lutea* and *P. potaninii* are considered to fall within the natural variability of *P. delavayi*).

> subsection *Vaginatae* Flowers solitary, mostly 5 carpels.
> Seven species, including the most renowned of all peonies, *P. rockii*.

section Onaepia

Herbaceous perennials, petals nearly equal to or smaller than sepals.
Two North American species, *P. brownii* and *P. californica*.

section Paeonia

Herbaceous perennials, petals much larger than sepals.

> subsection *Albiflorae*
> Found in Asia, with *P. anomala* extending into north-eastern Europe. Carrot-shaped roots and usually several flowers per stem or solitary, with undeveloped flower buds at axils. Four species, *P. lactiflora*,

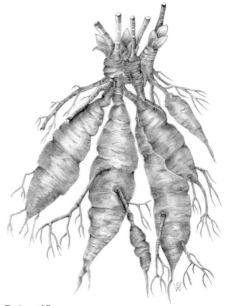

P. lactiflora

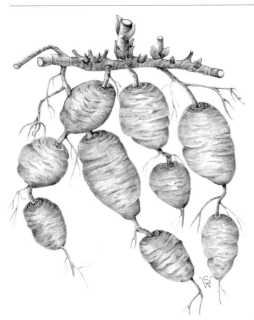

P. tenuifolia

subsection *Paeonia*
From Central Asia to northern
Mediterranean. Roots fusiform
or tuberous. Lower leaves
usually have 21-340 leaflets.
Solitary flowers. Seven species
including *P. tenuifolia*, *P.
peregrina*, *P. arietina* and *P.
officinalis*.

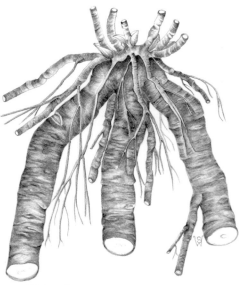

P. officinalis

P. emodi, *P. sterniana* and *P.
anomala*.

subsection *Foliolatae*
Found in East Asia and in
Europe, NW Africa and from
Western Mediterranean to
Iran. Carrot-shaped roots.
Lower leaves usually 9-21
leaflets (more in *P. broteri* and
P. clusii). Solitary flowers.
Eleven species including *P.
obovata*, *P. cambessedesii*, *P.
daurica* (and its subspecies
mlokosewitschii) and *P. mascula*.

P. tenuifolia

HYBRID PEONIES

The best-known hybrid peony is the tree peony *P. suffruticosa*. This is the name given to plants derived from several species of the subsection *Vaginatae* and so can be applied to any of the traditional ornamental tree peony cultivars such as 'Hei Hua Kui' and 'Cardinal Vaughan'. *P. lemoinei* takes its name from the French company Lemoine who in the early 20th century did much work crossing *P. suffruticosa* cultivars with *P. delavayi* (in the yellow form, then known as *P. lutea*) in subsection *Delavayanae*. The famous plant 'Souvenir de Maxime Cornu' raised by Louis Henry is an example of this cross. Unfortunately many of the cultivars inherited a tendency from their delavayi parent to hold the flowers on nodding stems, which means they can get somewhat lost among the foliage.

The term hybrid peonies is often used to group those herbaceous plants derived from crosses between the Chinese lactifloras and species such as *P. officinalis* and *P. peregrina*. These often combine the rich colours of their European ancestors with the more generous flower count of the Chinese plants. Plants with this background, such as 'Buckeye Belle' or the recent introduction 'Cherry Ruffles', make wonderful garden plants.

The most exciting hybrids are the Itoh peonies which are intersectional hybrids between section *Moutan* and section *Paeonia*, first achieved by Toichi Itoh, a Japanese nurseryman. Itoh pollinated thousands of peonies before, in 1948, successfully crossing the Lemoine hybrid tree peony 'Alice Harding' with a double white lactiflora called 'Kakoden'. Thirty-six seedlings resulted, of which nine looked like tree peonies whilst the others were more herbaceous in character. Sadly Itoh died before his seedlings flowered, but Shigao-Oshida, his son-in-law, continued to look after them and they started to flower in 1963. The plants were purchased from Itoh's widow in 1966 by Louis Smirnow of New York who registered the best of them with the American Peony Society in 1974 as 'Yellow Crown', 'Yellow Dream', 'Yellow Emperor' and 'Yellow Heaven'.

A number of breeders in America have continued Itoh's work and are introducing many excellent plants. Most modern cultivars are still very expensive but mature quickly to form substantial specimen plants, showing hybrid vigour. They have a neat habit, creating low, spreading bushes with shoots that are usually herbaceous. The attractive foliage looks like that of tree peonies and has good disease resistance. They flower over an extended period, with mature plants in bloom for around four weeks and occasionally re-blooming later in the season. The large flowers come in a range of spectacular colours. Flowers from side buds may vary in colour and shape from the terminal flowers, giving a wonderful kaleidoscope effect.

CLASSIFICATION OF FLOWERS

Various systems of classification have been used to help describe the differing flower shapes. Bear in mind that the shapes of some peony flowers can vary depending on the maturity of the plant and the season. For example, the flowers of 'Chocolate Soldier' can appear single or Japanese, and many double peonies have semi-double side buds.

Single

A ring of 5-13 petals surrounding functional stamens and carpels. Examples: 'Scarlet O'Hara', 'White Wings', 'Avant Garde'.

'Avant Garde'

Japanese

Sometimes called imperial peonies, these have an outer ring of normal petals, referred to as the guard petals. Most of the stamens are converted into narrow, ribbon-like staminodes. Anemone-flowered forms are similar but the stamens have become broader and more petal-like. Examples: 'Bowl of Beauty', 'Do Tell', 'White Cap'.

'White Cap'

Semi-double

Several rows of petals but usually have functional carpels and stamens. Examples: 'Coral Charm', 'Cytherea', 'Rosedale'.

'Coral Charm'

Double

All the stamens and carpels have developed into petals resembling those of the outer ring. Examples: 'Albert Crousse', 'Festiva Maxima' 'Sarah Bernhardt'.

'Sarah Bernhardt'

Bomb

Both carpels and stamens have developed into broad petals but the outer ring of guard petals is still clearly differentiated. Examples: 'Sorbet', 'Félix Crousse', 'Red Charm'.

'Sorbet'

Cultivation

PURCHASE AND PLANTING

Peonies are popular and extremely long-lived plants and many gardeners who grow peonies did not actually buy their plants but inherited them from a previous owner of their home or indeed from a parent or grandparent. Most commonly seen is the double red 'Rubra Plena', a cultivar or hybrid of *P. officinalis*, which is often called the cottage garden peony because it is seen so often in the informal borders of small gardens. It is able to survive years of neglect and yet, with just a little care, can produce a really impressive specimen plant.

Individual peony plants can live for more than 50 years and so, although perhaps initially expensive, they can be viewed as an excellent investment. This can be your excuse to justify any new acquisitions to sceptical, non-gardening partners, but a certain level of scepticism is also a beneficial quality in the would-be peony purchaser. Over the years many peony cultivars have become hopelessly muddled in the nursery trade, and even when buying from specialist suppliers you may sometimes find that the plant purchased bears little relation to what is written on the label. However, the specialist peony grower can usually be depended upon to put right any such errors and to supply good quality, healthy plants. Plants bought from general garden centres have often been imported from the Netherlands as bare-rooted plants in the autumn, and then potted up into pots of cheap, peat-based composts and grown on for sale in the spring. Peat is not really a suitable growing material for peonies, aside from any ecological considerations, because it can retain too much water, and if peonies are left sitting for months in a cold, soggy medium, rots can develop.

Plants ordered from specialist growers will usually be delivered in the autumn and should be planted as soon as possible. This allows them to get established and to develop new feeding roots before the winter sets in. However, if gardening in wet areas or on very heavy soil, it may be better to over-winter the new purchases in pots of a well-drained gritty compost, and plant out when the new growth is beginning in the spring. If you have been tempted by a cheap, potted peony it may be best, whatever the time of year, to tip it out of the pot, gently shake off any compost, and examine the roots carefully; if they look healthy, then plant it out in the garden or into a pot of more suitable compost. If, however, there are any signs of rot, cut back to healthy tissue, sprinkle with sulphur powder and re-pot. Keep the compost on the dry side until the plant has had a chance to heal over.

Choose the planting site with care. Avoid areas which accumulate standing water in the winter. The majority of peonies, especially the popular lactiflora cultivars, will flower most generously in a site that receives at least six hours of sunlight a day. Species such as *P. anomala* subsp. *veitchii*, *P. daurica* subsp. *mlokosewitschii*, *P. mascula*, *P. peregrina* and the Wind-flower hybrids, flower well in the dappled shade of trees and shrubs, as do most tree peonies, but no peonies will flourish in really dense shade. Do not plant too close to trees such as poplar and willow which have very greedy roots. Peonies are lime-tolerant and will grow in any fertile, well-drained soil. In Luoyang, which is one of the major tree peony growing regions of China, they flourish in loess soils with a high mineral content and a pH of around 7.2.

Tree peonies are very cold-hardy and in their native China will survive temperatures down to -20°C. However, when considering hardiness it is not just a question of minimum temperatures. A plant growing in an area with hot, sunny summers will be better able to ripen the shoots and so subsequently tolerate lower temperatures than one in which the wood has not lignified sufficiently. Late frosts can also badly damage young growth, so try to avoid frost pockets. Japanese-style peony shelters can be created from coppiced willow stems and straw to provide protection for treasured young plants.

Shelter for a peony using willow stems and straw

The large-flowered tree peonies and double-flowered forms of herbaceous peonies can easily be battered by wind during the flowering season, so consider some form of wind protection. For very windy gardens, select shorter-growing cultivars. In the United States, some breeders are developing a range of short, 'rock-garden peonies' which do not require staking. For example, the white-flowered 'Squirt' and the red 'Happy', both from Roy Klehm, bloom at up to 40cm. In the UK you should be able to find 'Little Medicine Man' and 'Anemoniflora Rosea' which grow to 50-60cm.

Dig a decent-sized planting hole, at least 40-50 cm deep. Herbaceous peonies are generally supplied as divisions with three to five eyes or buds. Plant them out so that the buds are 5cm below the soil level. Planting too deeply insulates the crown from winter chilling and summer warmth which are necessary to initiate formation of flower buds. Back-fill the hole with the topsoil mixed with some well-rotted compost, and firm the soil around the roots. Do not use fresh manure near the peony crown.

Water the plants thoroughly and repeat regularly during the first growing season to encourage deep rooting. After a couple of years the peonies will develop substantial storage roots and will show good drought tolerance but they do need to be reasonably moist in spring to help the production of good flowers. Peonies will flower after a dry spring, but the flowering period can be greatly reduced. On light soils and in dry climates they may benefit from a mulch in the spring to help keep the roots cool and moist. However, take care to ensure that mulching material does not pile up around the stems as this can encourage fungal growth. Birds, particularly blackbirds, are notorious for flicking mulches around.

Peonies are long-lived plants and so it is worth investing in decent labels that will endure throughout their lifetime. Plastic labels deteriorate and become brittle after exposure to sunlight, so it is preferable to choose permanent labels, such as those made from aluminium or copper, which can have the plant name etched into them. Labels do have a tendency to walk, so it is a good idea also to keep a plan of your garden with the location of your peonies marked on it.

Patience is required whilst new peony plants mature. It is sometimes suggested that you remove the first year's flower buds so that the plant can put its energies into getting established but I am not convinced that it really makes much difference. Cynics say that suppliers suggest this so that purchasers do not realise they have a misnamed plant until it is too late to complain, but in any case it is best not to be too hasty about complaining, as the first year's flowers may not be typical of the cultivar, and it is not unusual for double cultivars to show single or semi-double flowers until they settle down.

Tree peonies are sometimes thought to be difficult to grow. Indeed, back in 1890 William Watson wrote in the magazine *Garden and Forest* that the plants die a foot for every six inches they grow. Tree peonies on their own roots are usually very vigorous, but unfortunately the majority are sold grafted onto an herbaceous rootstock. Suppliers usually recommend that the peony is planted deeply, so that the graft union is approximately 15cm below the soil surface. This aims to encourage the scion to produce its own roots and the rootstock to shrivel away; this may indeed happen successfully, but on other occasions the rootstock may send up suckers which compete with the scion for water and nutrients. This can happen as many as ten years after the peony was planted. Alternatively, a formerly healthy tree peony may start to deteriorate, and on digging it up to investigate, a large swollen mass of callus tissue is found at the graft site.

It is recommended that grafted plants be lifted and examined after two or three years. If the plant has a reasonable quantity of roots above the graft point, all the herbaceous rootstock should be cut away and the peony replanted. Plants that have not developed scion roots should be replanted and examined again in another year or two.

GOOD COMPANIONS

Peonies do not like to be crowded but this does not mean that they have to be planted in splendid isolation. They can be combined happily with many other plants, but try to avoid anything too vigorous that would swamp the peony crown. Small spring bulbs such as snowdrops, crocus, reticulata irises,

'Buckeye Belle' shoots

chionodoxa and miniature narcissi, for example 'Segovia', all make enchanting companions to the lovely red-bronze new shoots of peonies at the start of the year.

As they come into flower, peonies combine well with bearded and sibirica irises, which provide contrasting foliage shape and colours. Other blue-flowered plants, such as *Centaurea montana*, *Aconitum* 'Spark's Variety', and the Dutch irises 'Frans Hals' and 'Professor Blaauw', work well with almost any colour of peony. The deep red peonies such as 'Buckeye Belle' and 'Burma Ruby' are lovely seen through a haze of purple fennel with dark astrantias. Dicentras and *Lamprocapnos spectabilis* (formerly *Dicentra spectabilis*), aquilegias, epimediums and violas are also suitable companions.

Lilies, such as *Lilium candidum*, or galtonias are ideal to follow on, once the peonies have finished their display. Colchicums also work well, often flowering at the same time as the peony leaves start to colour and their seed pods open, to add a final interest to the peony season.

MAINTENANCE

Dead-heading peonies as the flowers fade does not, unfortunately, encourage them to produce a second flush of flowers. There is a school of thought that dead-heading saves the plants expending energy on producing seed, and enables them to give a better display the following year, but observations reported by the American Peony Society show that allowing plants to set seed does not make an appreciable difference to flower production the following year. In wet weather, some of the big double flowers do not drop their petals cleanly and they can start to decay on the stem. In such cases dead-heading is obviously beneficial, but otherwise just enjoy the added interest of the developing seedpods.

Some peonies have leaves that take on attractive autumn colours, particularly in years in which the nights are cold but the days still warm. They can start to change colour earlier than many other herbaceous plants - around the middle of August - whereas other cultivars may not turn until October. Some cultivars just turn into a dull and unappealing brown, but others, such as 'Doreen' and 'Cream Puff', can turn a good red.

As this final display of the year ends, in September or October, cut off and bin

Autumn colour on tree peony

fertilisers. However, on light soils they will benefit from a slow-release fertiliser such as bonemeal or pelleted chicken manure applied in autumn, and a handful of rose fertiliser sprinkled around each crown in March. A couple of applications of high potassium, tomato-type liquid feed during the growing season will encourage flowering and is said to make plants less prone to *Botrytis*.

Established plants are unlikely to need much in the way of watering, although in dry springs they will flower better if irrigated. A good drenching is more beneficial than watering little and often. If you wish to save seed from your plants, watering will be important for those plants carrying a heavy seed set. When watering, try to avoid wetting the foliage, to reduce the likelihood of fungal infections.

or burn all foliage. This will ensure that any fungal spores present on the leaves do not stay around to infect the next season's new shoots. Scrape any moss from the crown and cover exposed crowns with soil or leaf mould. Any holes in the peony crowns should be filled with gritty soil or they will become home to slugs and woodlice.

Feeding and watering

On fertile clay soils, peonies can grow for many years without additional

Staking

Whether or not you need to stake your peonies depends on which varieties you grow, the situation in which you grow them and your style of gardening. Some gardeners like their plants to stand to attention whereas others prefer a more casual look, with their peonies leaning companionably on other plants. Plants growing in an open sunny site will be less likely to need support than those leaning towards the sun because they are growing against a wall or hedge. However, plants in exposed sites may suffer more from wind damage.

Plants with heavy double flowers are more likely to need staking, but it is not just a matter of the weight of the flower. Some cultivars, such as the very old lactiflora 'Duchesse de Nemours', have stems that if left unsupported will usually be flat on the ground well before the flower buds even begin to open. Many of the newer hybrids, such as 'Etched Salmon', 'Paula Fay' and 'Pink Hawaiian Coral', have been bred

to have sturdier stems and so should not need staking.

The new bronze shoots of peonies are visually very attractive and form a lovely backdrop to early spring bulbs, so it is a shame to insert stakes too early. However, when peonies start to shoot up, they can grow extremely quickly, and it then becomes difficult to stake them without causing damage. The best time is probably when the shoots are 15-20cm tall and before the leaves start to expand.

Do not truss the plants too tightly, or the inner leaves will harbour damp

A staking system using flexible tubing

and may fall victim to fungal attack. It is better to let the clumps splay out slightly, to allow good air circulation. Several different staking methods are used, from bamboo canes supporting a cat's cradle of strong garden twine, to pea sticks or metal plant supports with a wire grid that the plant grows through. Cylinders of wire fencing, concrete remesh, or tomato cages are effective, but can look intrusive. The plastic posts used to support electric fencing are easy to push into the soil and can be used with loops of clear, flexible tubing. Low box hedging may be sufficient to stop peonies flopping over a path.

Weeding

If weeds are allowed to grow in the peony beds they will compete for water and nutrients, shade the roots and, by decreasing air circulation, increase the risk of fungal infections. Winter-green weeds can be sprayed with a glyphosate-based weedkiller while the peonies are dormant, but during the growing season great care must be taken that no spray drifts onto the peony foliage. Peonies that have been inadvertently sprayed may not necessarily die, but can show distorted and discoloured leaves and greatly reduced growth. It is safer, though obviously time-consuming, to hand-weed. If a hoe is used, take care not to damage young buds when working near the peony crown.

Some members of the HPS Peony Group have come up with ingenious methods of weed-control over the years. A commercial grower in New Zealand sends in 50 lambs to her peony fields during the growing season. They dislike the taste of green peony leaves but will carefully eat any weeds growing between the plants. At the end of the season, when the leaves have gone brown, the lambs are returned, and will then clear up the brown leaves and stems. In Finland, ducks and geese are used to keep peony beds free of couch grass and dandelions. The ducks also clear the ground of any slugs and snails. A goose is a better guard than any dog, and as well as clearing weeds, can be a useful ally to those who have problems with plant theft. Of course, using animals for weed control has the additional benefit of keeping the soil fertility up.

Transplanting

Peonies can be grown undisturbed in the same position for many years without problems. However, there may be occasions when you wish to transplant a peony, such as when a border is to be redesigned, or even when moving house and wanting to take a treasured plant with you. The ideal time for transplanting is the autumn, but if this is not possible, then do it at any time. Peonies moved in full growth may sulk for a while but should recover.

The ground should be reasonably moist, but if not, give the plant a couple of bucketfuls of water the night before you dig it up. In late summer or autumn, cut the peony stems down to near ground level. Earlier in the year, it is worth retaining some foliage, but reduce the leaf area by around two-thirds. Carefully dig around and under the plant, trying to retain as much of the root system as possible.

If the plant is to be replanted immediately, place it in a prepared hole ensuring that the crown is not more than 5cm below the soil surface. Backfill the hole with soil or a soil and compost mix, then water thoroughly. If you are unable to replant straight away, the peonies can be kept temporarily in large pots, plastic crates, or root-control bags, as sold by tree and fruit nurseries.

Old plants will often benefit from being divided into sections rather than replanted in their entirety; this seems to reinvigorate them, and of course means that you have more plants for yourself or to share with friends. When dividing the plants, try to ensure that each division has at least three eyes and a good portion of the root system. They should then establish quickly and start flowering again within a year or two.

Pruning tree peonies

Tree peony plants are usually expensive, and have such impressive flowers that gardeners tend to be rather timid about pruning them for fear of killing them, or at least spoiling subsequent displays. If a tree peony is growing well, flowering regularly, and has not outgrown the space available to it, then there is certainly no need to prune it. However, as with other woody shrubs, pruning can often be beneficial. Always ensure that secateurs and/or pruning saw are clean, and when pruning more than one plant, it is worth regularly flaming the blade with a match or lighter to ensure that you do not pass any fungal or viral diseases between plants.

For the first couple of years after planting, while the plant is establishing a good root system, prune solely to remove any dead wood. However, if after three to four years from planting, there are only one or two spindly stems, then it is worth cutting the peony down to ground level in autumn. Give it a top-dressing of bone meal and ensure that the soil is reasonably moist. The plant should then respond with the production of a number of strong, vigorous stems to give a good, multi-branched specimen.

For established plants, remove any dead wood in late winter, cutting back to a healthy bud. If a whole branch has died, cut it down to ground level. Tree peony stems can be quite brittle, and are easily broken by stray footballs or other garden hazards. Broken stems should be cut back to the next set of leaves or right down to ground level to make a clean cut which will be less vulnerable to fungal attack. Plants that are becoming leggy can be pruned to stimulate a more branching, floriferous plant. Cut back all stems by a third as soon as they have finished flowering or, if you are feeling brave, cut the whole plant down to ground level in the winter. This will stimulate a lot of new growth, so make sure that the plant has enough water and feed to sustain it.

Chinese cultivars such as 'Hei Hua Kui', tend naturally to form low, rounded bushes, and so are less likely to require pruning than many of the Japanese suffruticosa cultivars which can get quite leggy. Some tree peonies, particularly the yellow-flowering *P. ludlowii*, are very vigorous, and can reach huge proportions. If you want to keep such plants to a more manageable size, prune them in summer, immediately after they have finished flowering. Remove any thick old stems and shorten other stems by a third to a half. Old plants that have become a congested mess of branches should be treated similarly to avoid *Botrytis* infection due to poor air circulation around the plant.

Pruning schedules that consistently take out one third of the oldest stems each autumn result in regular renewal of young wood, giving plants that produce fewer, but larger flowers - ideal if you want flowers for exhibition.

PEONIES IN POTS
It has often been said that you cannot grow peonies in pots, but the people who say this have presumably not been to an Alpine Garden Society show in the spring and gazed with awe at the pot-grown *P. cambessedesii* plants that sometimes grace the show benches. In China and Japan, tree peonies are often grown in pots, and make stunning specimen plants in a courtyard setting.

Peonies can in fact be grown successfully in pots for several years, but this requires an understanding of their needs. Unglazed terracotta pots tend to be the most satisfactory as they are permeable to moisture and air. It is important that they are of sufficient size to accommodate the peony roots easily and to allow for a couple of years growth. For a specimen plant, this usually means a pot with an internal diameter of at least 30cm. Pots with parallel, rather than the usual tapering sides, are more stable, but can be difficult to obtain.

The main difficulty is in getting a suitable potting mixture. Peonies need a fertile, but well-draining growing medium, open to the passage of oxygen, water and nutrients. The usual multi-purpose compost, whether peat-based or peat-free, tends to dry out too rapidly in summer and to be too wet in winter. Soil-based composts of the John Innes type are more tolerant of over- and under-watering and have better nutrient-holding capacities. However, they can vary greatly, even between batches from the same manufacturer, with some setting to a concrete-like consistency after a year or two. It is therefore difficult to make any specific recommendations and it may be better to make up a mixture of the two types with added grit or perlite to keep the mixture open to air and water.

Pot-grown plants are reliant on the gardener to provide water and nutrients, and will need additional feeding. The easiest way to do this is to give a tomato-type liquid feed once a month during the growing season. These feeds are rich in potassium, which promotes flowering. When using artificial fertilisers regularly, a build-up of salts can occur. Give a thorough watering with rain water from time to time to flush out accumulated salts. In areas which have severe winters it may be necessary to move the pots to an airy shed or garage or to insulate them with a layer of straw or bubble wrap so that the roots do not freeze solid.

If, after a few years of pot culture, a peony starts to deteriorate, remove it from the pot and gently shake or wash off the compost from the roots. Check for the presence of soil pests such as swift moth larvae (see below). Cut away any signs of rot in the root and dust with sulphur. Transplant into a larger pot if necessary, or divide the plant and return one division to the original container using fresh compost.

PESTS AND DISEASES

Peonies contain high levels of phenols, which taste disgusting, so garden pests such as deer and rabbits will not eat them. Moles will not eat peony roots, although they can undermine them with their tunnelling. Even aphids, slugs and snails will usually avoid them. Gardeners are sometimes worried about ants on their peonies. The flower buds of peonies produce a form of nectar that is very attractive to ants. This is thought to be so that the ants will protect the buds from other insect predators. Once the flowers open the ants usually disappear.

A particular pest is the Ghost Swift Moth, *Hepialus humuli*, the larvae of which are polyphagous and feed on the roots of several agricultural and horticultural crops. In Holland, it is known as the lettuce root-driller, as it was first found in lettuce crops in the early 1900s. It causes significant problems in the Dutch cut-flower industry. Adult swift moths are unlikely to be seen unless you are prone to night-time prowling around your garden. They spend the daylight hours concealed in vegetation and fly mostly on warm nights from June to August. The male moth earns its common name

Ants on bud of *Paeonia peregrina*

from its ghostly-white appearance, but the female is buff-coloured, and deposits her eggs in flight. The larvae are ugly white grubs with brown heads and around twice the length of vine weevil larvae. On hatching, they burrow in the ground where they feed on the roots of dandelions, coltsfoot and many other plants. Any new plants purchased or received should have their

biological approach is to treat with a spray of *Beauveria bassiana*, a fungal parasite of many arthropod species.

Various nematodes may attack peonies. These pests are soil-dwelling, worm-like creatures, usually less than 1mm long. Affected plants will show stunted growth and early leaf fall. There are no chemical controls currently available

Larva of the
Ghost Swift Moth

roots inspected for grubs. As with vine weevils, the larvae can be controlled using systemic insecticides containing imidacloprid, such as Provado Ultimate Bug Killer. However, great care must be taken with such products, as they are toxic to bees. Do not use insecticides whilst the peonies are in flower. The

for amateur use and affected plants should be burnt.

The most common disease of peonies is peony blight, caused by the fungus *Botrytis paeoniae*. Infection is most likely to occur in damp conditions and shows itself by a sudden wilting of stems and buds. Affected areas quickly shrivel and turn brown. The fungus overwinters as black, seed-like structures called sclerotia, in the dead tissue, becoming active again in the spring. Spores can travel long distances on the wind. Infection can be minimised by good garden hygiene, making sure that all peony stems and leaves are cleared up at the end of the season. Avoid planting peonies in heavy shade, allow plenty of air circulation around the plants, and prune tree peonies to maintain an open shape. Ensure plants are well nourished, as a lack of potassium in plant tissue makes them more vulnerable. Be vigilant in wet conditions, and at the first sign of *Botrytis* cut out and destroy the affected parts, disinfecting secateurs between plants. Scrape away the topsoil around affected plants and dust the remaining stems and tubers with sulphur dust before replacing with fresh, uninfected soil. If using mulches, keep them well away from the crown of the plant.

Another fungal disease is leaf blotch, or peony measles, caused by *Cladosporium paeoniae*, but this is more common in North America. It causes dark purple spots on the surfaces of the leaves, and streaks on young stems.

Crown rot can be caused by soil-borne fungi and bacteria, and is most likely to occur in waterlogged soil. Investigating a collapsed plant may reveal a black and rotting root system. Any healthy part of the crown can be cleaned up and

Botrytis paeoniae infection

dusted with sulphur, and may re-grow if planted in a well-drained position.

If you have had outbreaks of fungal disease, a protective spray is recommended in future seasons. The recent withdrawal of a number of pesticides previously available to the amateur gardener has made control of many fungal infections difficult. Do check current regulations before using any chemicals. Copper sulphate (Bordeaux mixture) is still available for the control of *Botrytis* on some fruit and vegetables, but this does not extend to use on ornamentals. The fungicides myclobutanil, available as Systhane Fungus Fighter, and penconazole, available as Scotts Fungus Clear, can be used to control other diseases on ornamental plants, and may provide incidental control against *Botrytis* and *Cladosporium*.

CUT FLOWERS

Peonies make wonderful cut-flowers, with an opulence that few other flowers can match. Fragrant cultivars such as 'Big Ben' and 'Vivid Rose' are particularly treasured. Cut peonies tend to be expensive to buy, particularly the more unusual cultivars such as 'Coral Charm' and the cherry-red, semi-double 'Cytherea', but are easy and very satisfying to grow yourself. If planting peonies specifically for cutting, choose an open sunny position away from competing tree roots. Make sure the plants are well fed with bonemeal or pelleted chicken manure in the autumn and give an application of sulphate of potash in the spring to encourage flowering.

Home gardeners may stake their peonies to ensure that the stems grow upright, but commercial growers, with many acres of plants to look after, obviously cannot do so. As garden plants, cultivars that produce many side buds are desirable, but for cut-flowers it is better to remove all the side buds. This allows the plant to concentrate its energies in developing the terminal bud, giving a bigger, better-quality flower. The earlier disbudding is carried out, the more effective it is. It is a fairly unpleasant job as the buds tend to be sticky.

Cut the flowers at what is known as the 'soft bud' stage, when the buds are full and the outer petals start to show through the sepals. When gently pinched, the bud should give slightly, somewhat like a marshmallow. Buds picked too early, when they are still hard, are unlikely to open. Remember that the plant needs to keep some leaves to build up reserves for next year, so if you want all the flowers, do not cut the stems too long, and ensure the plant retains at least half its leaf area. Strip the lower leaves from the stems and stand the flowers up to their necks in a bucket of water for a couple of hours or overnight.

Cut peonies do not do well arranged in Oasis. The flowers are very thirsty, and do better immersed in tall vases of water, which will need regularly topping up. Most peonies will last from five to seven days in a vase, although some, such as 'Qing Wen', last for ten days. Cultivars which scatter their petals relatively quickly are best displayed in flat dishes. Be aware that some of the red cultivars, for example 'Red Charm', can easily lose the pigment from their petals, and fallen petals may stain carpets.

Peonies travel well if kept cool at the bud stage, and commercial growers find them easy to package for transport around the world. Huge acres of peonies are grown for cut-flowers in the Netherlands and New Zealand. If stems are picked when the bud is well-developed but still firm, they can be stored at 0°C for up to six weeks,

extending the period over which they can be sold. In the home environment, if you want peonies for a special event you can store them in a spare domestic refrigerator for around four weeks. Cut the flowers with fairly short stems of around 30cm. Remove most of the leaves and wrap the base of the stem with some barely moist paper towel. Seal the flowers in large, zip-loc plastic bags and store in the refrigerator at between 0°C and 4°C. Check regularly to make sure that condensation is not building up in the bags, as this can encourage fungal growth. When you take the peonies out of storage, rinse them with water, re-cut the ends, and stand them in a bucket of water in a cool, shaded place to allow the buds to open slowly. So long as the blooms are kept cool, they should last as long as freshly-cut flowers.

Peonies can also be used for dried flowers. They should be cut when the flowers have fully opened and any dew evaporated, tied in bunches of up to six blooms, and hung upside down in a warm, dark, airy place. Red and deep pink flowers are most successful, retaining their colours well.

Propagation

SEED

Peonies are very easy to grow from seed, but the most important requirement will be patience, as it can often take five years or more from sowing the seed to seeing the first flower. The long wait is usually worthwhile, but do remember that there will inevitably be some variation among plants raised from seed, so the results might not be quite what you expect. This is particularly the case with plants raised from the seed of cultivated peonies, as cross-pollination may often occur between different cultivars growing together in the garden.

Peony seeds are relatively large and easy to handle. They range in size from those of *P. tenuifolia*, which are about 5mm long and look somewhat like chunky mice droppings, to those of the shrubby *P. ludlowii*, which are approximately 14mm long and appear more like broad beans. Fertile peony seeds can be brown, black or bluish in colour. Any bright scarlet seeds found in seed pods will be infertile, so do not waste

Seed pods of *Paeonia mascula*. Only the black seeds are viable

time sowing them. You occasionally hear gardeners recommending that seed should be tested in water before sowing – the theory being that viable seed sinks whilst dead seed floats. With peonies however, "it ain't necessarily so", and floating seed may actually germinate.

Peony seed is shed naturally in late summer or autumn, and there will often be a period of some weeks in which warm moist conditions encourage the development of the root. However, a period of winter chilling is normally required before the shoot develops, and the first leaf is seen as the weather warms again in the spring. Some seed will take more than two years before the first leaf is visible, so do not be in too much of a hurry to dispose of pots of apparently failed seed. Most peony species exhibit what is known as hypogeal germination, in which the cotyledons or seed leaves are retained within the seed coat, and it is the first true leaves that emerge above ground. Exceptions include *P. tenuifolia* and the North American *P. brownii*, which produce long, thin cotyledons before the first true leaves.

Generally speaking, peony seed will germinate best if sown fresh from the plant when it matures in late summer. However, seed that has been dried, such as commercial seed or that obtained from seed exchanges, will often still germinate successfully, although it may take longer to do so. Seed of some species, for example *P. tenuifolia*, can germinate surprisingly rapidly, even after two or more years of dry storage.

Mature seed contains germination inhibitors which prevent it from germinating until conditions are likely to be optimal for growth. If you collect the seed when it has fully developed but not yet ripened, you can catch it before the chemical inhibitors have been produced, and so the seed can germinate immediately; this can save a season's growing time. There is a bit of an art to knowing when to collect, but if you have plenty of seed set, particularly on tree peonies, you can experiment with gently squeezing the pods once they have fattened but are still green. Pods which split easily and contain seeds that are a mottled brown colour can be harvested for sowing.

In *The Book of Tree Peonies*, Gian Lupo Osti reports that at the Peony Research Institute in China, seeds of woody peonies are collected as soon as the pods open and are sown in August, before they dry out. This gives a germination percentage of 70-80%. The seedlings are transplanted after three years and the first blooms usually appear four or five years (range 3-7 years) after germination.

Peony seedlings are slow to mature, so it is better to use loam-based sowing compost, which retains its structure better than one composed predominantly of peat. However, many such types of compost can set like concrete after a year or two, so it is advisable to mix in a proportion of grit, which will ensure that the compost remains free-draining and porous to air. Horticultural grit or the flint grit sold by corn merchants for chickens, used in a ratio of one part grit to around three parts compost, usually gives good results. Sow the seed in pots large enough to provide a stable environment: a 15cm pot is sufficient for around a dozen seeds. Cover the seeds in their own depth of compost and top with a layer of grit to reduce the growth of lichens. Water well, and place the pots outside, exposed to the weather, to stimulate germination.

Seedlings should usually be left in the same pot for at least a year after germination. They can then be potted up individually into a gritty compost and grown on for a year or two before planting out. If you have a lot of seed available, it can be sown in rows in any prepared bed of well-drained soil. Peony seedlings do not usually need a lot of attention, apart from removing weeds, which compete for water and nutrients. However, if some appear not to be thriving, it is worth tipping them out of the pot to check for the presence of soil pests, such as the larvae of swift moth.

When the transplanted seedlings start to flower, the first blooms may not be typical of the mature flower, so do not be in a hurry to discard a disappointing new seedling. First flowers may well be single, but in subsequent years Japanese forms or even doubles could develop.

DIVISION

Division is the accepted method of propagation for herbaceous cultivars. It produces new plants, identical to the parent, and so long as the resulting divisions are large enough, plants usually recover quickly and may even flower the next year. Division can also be used for plants of herbaceous species, but if large quantities of plants are required they are often propagated by seed. However, seed produced by species plants in cultivation may be of hybrid origin if other peonies are grown nearby.

Many woody peonies can also be propagated by division, and Chinese growers frequently use this method, although in recent years they have been moving over to the Japanese method of grafting onto herbaceous rootstocks. Itoh hybrids inherit characteristics from both their herbaceous and woody parents and tend to develop rootstocks that are intermediate between the two. They are usually propagated by division, but heavy tools and considerable energy may be required to divide the massive woody rootstocks.

The best time to divide peonies is in the autumn, so that they have the winter to re-establish a network of feeding roots before the buds start to develop in springtime. If the soil is dry, it is beneficial to give the plant a couple of bucketfuls of water the night before dividing it. It is easiest to cut down the stems before dividing the plant. Dig around the outside of the peony with a spade or fork then lever it up, trying not to damage the central crown. Old plants have quite brittle roots and are likely to sustain some damage. If soil clings to the crown and roots, hose them down, to more easily identify the eyes (new buds at the base of the stems, where next year's growth will come from). Eyes may be white or red, depending on cultivar, variable in size, and usually conical and shiny. Lifting a mature plant can sometimes take twenty minutes or more of serious digging and heaving. Once done, it is a good idea to leave the peony to settle for a couple of hours, as it then becomes less brittle and easier to cut.

Very long roots should be trimmed back to around 15cm. Sometimes plants will divide easily just by pulling them apart with your hands. If not, then with a sharp spade or strong knife, cut the crown into sections, aiming to divide into pieces with a minimum of 3-5 healthy buds and a similar number of strong roots. Smaller pieces, with just one bud and some root, will still grow, but will take longer to reach flowering size. The best, most vigorous plants will come from the outside of the crown; the central portion often becomes very woody and may be better discarded.

Any areas with black or soft rot should be cut back to healthy tissue. It is a sensible precaution to dust cut surfaces with sulphur to ward off fungal infections.

The roots of some peonies, such as *P. peregrina*, *P. officinalis* and *P. tenuifolia*, have adventitious buds which can develop into new plants. This can be seen when the herbaceous root stock of a grafted tree peony starts to send up shoots. If, on lifting a peony to divide it, pieces of root break off, it is worth potting them up or lining them out in the vegetable patch to see if they will grow (see p. 43). The high concentration of phenol compounds in peony roots makes them resistant to bacterial and fungal attack, so pieces left in the ground can remain there without rotting for a considerable time and can send up new shoots a couple of years after the original plant was lifted.

The divisions can be replanted straight away, but in a commercial setting, depending on the nursery and the postal service, plants may be out of the ground for at least a week without harm. If they are not to be replanted immediately, do not allow them to dry out completely; keep them in a cool, shady position, preferably wrapped in moss, or something similar to keep them fresh.

The methods described above are ideal, but of course few of us are ideal gardeners, and peonies are usually pretty tolerant of less-than-ideal treatment. Plants can be divided just as successfully in the spring, as growth restarts, although if conditions are dry they may require regular watering until the roots re-establish. In fact, if necessary, peonies can be divided in full growth, but do cut off all but the lowest leaf on each stem to reduce transpiration while they settle in again.

Digging up a treasured peony and taking a knife to it can take some nerve, as well as quite a lot of energy, and if you just want a couple of extra plants you can use a spade to chop a piece from the edge of a plant, leaving the main part untouched. Fill in the hole made with some good compost, and the original plant will come to no harm. I have done this successfully, even in the flowering season, when friends have visited and coveted a particular plant. Cut off the flowering stem and enjoy it in a vase, and plant the division out as soon as possible.

Do not divide peonies too frequently, as they need time to recover their energy reserves and grow new storage roots. In general, garden plants can be divided every four or five years, although commercially, they will be divided more frequently. If Itoh hybrids are left too long, the rootstocks become very woody and difficult to divide, so if you intend to propagate them, it is best to lift them every two or three years. Even so, they may require dividing with a saw or even a hammer and chisel.

Tree peonies of the Chinese type often send up multiple well-spaced stems from the base and these can be divided. Young vigorous plants of perhaps three or four years old, divide better than old woody plants that have been left for more than ten years. Lift when the plants become dormant in the autumn and hose off any soil from the roots. Plants can usually be pulled apart by hand, but try and ensure that, as with herbaceous divisions, there are three to five eyes to each new plant. If the plant has plenty of buds on the crown and roots, then it is best to cut off the stems to ground level before replanting, to encourage it to form a new, well-branched plant. Divisions should be planted out rather deeper than was the original plant, which also helps to encourage the crown to send up good vigorous new shoots.

LAYERING

Layering is a method of vegetative propagation by which stems are induced to form adventitious roots while still attached to the parent plant. They can then be detached and grown on individually. It is perfectly possible to layer tree peonies, but their branches tend to be brittle and easily broken, so it must be done with care. Plants growing next to a hedge or wall often lean out towards the light, and it may be possible to bend the shoots down to the soil level. Most success is achieved using vigorous new-season shoots encouraged by hard pruning in autumn or winter. The optimal time for layering is in early summer, during, or just after the flowering period.

Select a shoot and bend it down gently so that you can see at which point it will most easily touch the soil. The tip of the shoot needs to extend some 15cm or so beyond the point at which you peg it down. Ensure that the soil at that point is friable; dig it over with a trowel and add some good compost if required. Remove the leaf closest to the selected point, and at that axil cut off a sliver of bark to expose the cambium cells. Brush with hormone rooting powder or liquid and then peg down. Covering the stem with a heap of good soil or a rock helps to stimulate rooting. Constriction the stem by twisting copper wire into the tissue is also said to be beneficial. As the tip grows, tie it

Layering a shrubby peony

to a bamboo cane to make sure that it grows vertically. Layers will often take a year to start rooting and should be left for a further year, after which time they can be severed from the parent plant and grown on.

For larger quantities of new plants, a more drastic step is to cut the parent plant to the ground to stimulate the production of multiple young stems. Heap a large pile of good soil or compost over the crown to a depth of at least 15cm. New shoots should grow through and root into the mound and can be separated after two years. I suggest you practise this first on an unregarded plant.

CUTTINGS

One of the problems with growing tree peonies is their tendency to throw root suckers from the herbaceous rootstock on which most cultivars are grafted. Raising tree peonies from cuttings bypasses this problem as they will have their own roots. Peony cuttings are generally viewed as difficult, and therefore not good as a commercial method of propagation. However, for home gardeners who are prepared to accept a relatively low success rate, propagation by cuttings is the ideal way of producing more of their favourite tree peonies. Itoh hybrids can also be successfully raised from cuttings, thus avoiding the problem of having to lift these substantial plants for propagation by division.

Softwood cuttings taken from the first flush of new growth in spring or early summer have the greatest potential to form roots, but need to be maintained in humid conditions to ensure that they do not wilt, which means that they are also the most likely to succumb to fungal infections. Success is most likely with cuttings taken at around flowering time, when the growth is riper and so more resistant to attack. Cuttings taken by the beginning of June will have the best chance of forming adequate root systems to enable them to overwinter.

Take new shoots, ideally with a 'heel' of tissue from the last season's stem by carefully pulling the shoot downwards from the parent plant. Shorten the length of the shoot to around 10-15cm, cutting just above a leaf axil. Cuttings should have at least two buds. Reduce the leaf area to minimize evaporation. Use pots of a sterile, open, rooting medium such as a peat and sand mix (small quantities can be sterilised by pouring boiling water through and allowing it to drain). Dip each cutting into hormone rooting powder or solution and insert into the compost, ensuring that at least one bud is completely buried. Spray with a fungicide. Cover with a cut-down plastic soft drinks bottle to maintain humidity, but take it off from time to time so that the cuttings do not get too wet with condensation.

Use of a propagator with bottom heat may speed up rooting, but unfortunately also encourages the growth of moulds, which is the biggest problem with peony cuttings, and not easily controlled by fungicides available for amateur use. I have had the most success with cuttings lined out in a shady part of the vegetable patch with a cloche or an old propagator lid to protect them. A cold frame would provide a similar environment.

Cuttings can remain in a healthy-looking condition for a considerable time without actually forming roots, so do not be in too much of a hurry to tip them out of the pot. Remove the cover from potted cuttings if you see signs of new growth and do so anyway at the end of the summer, moving the pot into a sheltered place outside. Any green growth will die back in the autumn, but with luck you will see new buds forming in the spring. Pot up when the root system fills the current pot.

A rooted peony cutting

Members of The Peony Society have recently been experimenting with pre-treating cuttings by etiolation, according to an article in *The Plantsman* (Gunn, 2005), on the rooting of cuttings of lilac (*Syringa vulgaris*), which can be notoriously difficult. The research found that lilac cuttings taken from new shoots deprived of light form roots much more readily, and the roots themselves are more vigorous and fibrous. The article suggests cutting 2.5 x 2.5cm squares of black Velcro, dusting the inside with hormone rooting powder and fixing them around new shoots in spring (early April through to July, depending on cultivar). The important thing is to exclude light, so black duct tape or even stockings could be used instead. The covering is left on for 4 weeks, and cuttings are then taken from just below the area covered. Cuttings of *S. vulgaris* 'Michel Bucher' treated this way had 90-100% success rate compared with 0-50% for untreated cuttings. Preliminary results on tree peonies have been quite promising, and further experimentation is ongoing.

Putting a Velcro patch on a shoot to be taken as a cutting

McMillan Browse (2011) reports that the ability of the stem to initiate roots declines as the plant ages, so that cuttings from a cultivar such as 'Reine Elisabeth' from around 1895 may be more difficult to root than the cultivar 'Leda' raised by Daphnis in 1977. Manipulating stock plants by heavy pruning to stimulate the production of vigorous non-flowering shoots helps to maintain a higher level of regenerative ability.

Some herbaceous peonies may be propagated by root cuttings, as they naturally produce adventitious shoots from the roots (see p. 38). *P. peregrina*, and *P. officinalis*, and cultivars derived from these species, such as 'Burma Ruby', 'Crimson Globe' 'Lize van Veen', 'Paula Fay' and 'Salmon Glow', are ideal for this method. Root cuttings can be made if pieces of root break off during division. Alternatively, crowns can be specifically lifted for cuttings in late winter. Select cuttings of 10-15cm long and plant them in trenches in the open ground or in deep, 'Long Tom' type pots. It does not seem to matter whether you plant them vertically or lay them crossways in the trench. Some cuttings will have formed buds by the following autumn, but it may be necessary to wait until the year after before you see growing shoots.

GRAFTING

Grafting is usually used for the commercial production of tree peonies, as it enables more plants to be produced in a shorter time and at less expense than other methods. Herbaceous peony rootstocks are specially grown for the purpose, and scions of the desired tree peonies grafted onto them. Most suppliers sell the resulting plants with the herbaceous root still in place. The problem is that if the herbaceous rootstock remains, it may eventually start to produce its own shoots, which can overtake those of the desired plant. Also, incomplete compatibility between the rootstock and scion can lead to the development of a mass of dense tissue at the union site. However, if the herbaceous rootstock is treated as a temporary nurse root, and removed once the tree peony has grown enough roots of its own, then this can be an effective method of propagation (see p. 21).

Grafting may be a bit fiddly, but it can be managed by the amateur gardener. The best months for it are August and September, when the tree peony stems are mature, but not too woody, but it can be attempted at any time between mid-July and late autumn. When choosing the herbaceous root-stock, select a cultivar from *P. lactiflora* or *P.*

mascula, as they are less likely to produce adventitious buds than those with *P. officinalis* or *P. peregrina* in their breeding. Wash the roots clean and select chunky sections around 2cm in diameter and 15-20cm long, making sure you know which end is 'up' and which 'down'. Rub off any small hairy roots. Choose a stem from the tree peony to be propagated, and select scions of up to 15cm with 2-3 dormant buds in the leaf axils. Remove the leaves, and soak both scions and rootstocks in a dilute solution of household bleach (around 10% bleach in water) for a couple of hours.

Sterilise a cutting board and a sharp craft knife or razor blade with bleach or alcohol. Rinse the roots and scions, and for each root, trim the top and bottom to remove tissue that was in contact with the bleach. Then cut a cleft about 2.5cm long from the top end. Cut two slices from the base of the scion so that it fits into the cleft on the rootstock. When aligned, the green cambium layer just under the bark of the scion should be in contact with the cut surface of the root. Bind the two together with a piece of rubber band, and cover the join with grafting tape to prevent water getting in.

To allow the join to begin to callous over before planting, wrap the graft in damp kitchen towel and seal in a plastic bag; then place in a warm airing cupboard or greenhouse for around a month. The grafted roots can then be planted into deep 'Long Tom' pots or outdoors. Plant so that the graft union is at least 10cm below the soil level to encourage the tree peony to form its own roots. The soil or compost should be just slightly damp, not moist; outdoor plantings are best protected with a cloche until new shoots appear in the spring when the plant should be watered normally.

After two years, lift the plant to check for root growth. If the scion has produced its own roots, the nurse rootstock should be cut off and the peony potted up or planted out. Do not leave the herbaceous rootstock in place, as extensive callus formation can develop at the graft site, which in some cases can become football-sized, and can lead to the eventual death of the tree peony.

A German nurseryman is using the Itoh hybrid 'Bartzella' as rootstock for his tree peony grafts. He feels that the hybrid is more compatible with tree peonies owing to its mixed genetic makeup. Itoh hybrids can themselves be grafted in the same manner as above, although reports indicate a smaller percentage success rate than with tree peonies.

Directory of Peonies

AGM: RHS Award of Garden Merit

HERBACEOUS SPECIES AND CULTIVARS

P. anomala

A robust perennial, to 1.2m tall with thick taproots that can be up to 1m long. It grows mainly in forest and at forest edges and is widespread in China and Russia, preferring relatively moist soil. It has attractive leaves with narrow leaflets and usually just a solitary red or pink flower to each stem. The flowers nod at first, opening to flat saucers. The Chinese *P. veitchii* is now considered to be a subspecies of *P. anomala*, differing in that it usually has two to four flowers per stem.

P. brownii

One of only two American species, *P. brownii* is something of an oddity. It grows to around 45cm and has very attractive divided, glaucous leaves. The flowers are very small and the sepals are larger than the maroon-coloured petals. At first glance they resemble hellebore flowers. *P. brownii* is not often grown in the UK, and requires a very well-drained soil and plenty of sunshine. It is hardier than the other American species, *P. californica*, which differs in having less-divided leaves and usually three carpels, whereas *P. brownii* most often has five carpels.

Paeonia anomala subsp. *veitchii*

P. cambessedesii AGM

This lovely early-flowering species is endangered in the wild, being confined to just a few sites in the Balearic Islands. It grows to 45cm and has greyish-green leaves which are usually purple underneath. The flowers are pink and have up to eight carpels in the centre. It prefers a sunny, sheltered site in a well-drained gritty soil. Many alpine enthusiasts grow it in pots in the alpine house, and it can sometimes be seen at the spring shows of the Alpine Garden Society. Occasional white-flowering forms have been raised from seed.

Leaves of *Paeonia cambessedesii*

P. clusii

Endemic to Crete, Karpathos and Rhodes, *P. clusii* is rare in cultivation, but examples such as those in the Davis Alpine House at Kew Gardens and at the Chelsea Physic Gardens show how beautiful it can be. It has simple white or pink-tinged flowers held on purplish stems against smooth, hairless leaves. The filaments are red, contrasting well with the yellow anthers. It requires careful cultivation in dryish conditions.

P. daurica subsp. *mlokosewitschii* AGM

One of the most popular species peonies in cultivation is the lovely lemon-yellow *P. mlokosewitschii*, which is now considered to be one of seven subspecies of the variable *P. daurica*. It grows in deciduous forests on stony ground in Georgia, Azerbaijan and Russia, and wild populations have been found with very variable flower colours. Plants can be between 50cm and 1m in height. In the UK it usually flowers around the first week of May and will do well in full sun or woodland-type situations.

P. emodi

The Himalayan peony is an elegant species, generally growing to 60cm,

*Paeonia
daurica* subsp.
mlokosewitschii

although it can be up to 1m tall. It usually has two or three pure white flowers per stem. The flowers mostly have a single carpel. (The Windflower hybrids, which are often confused with *P. emodi*, can have one, two or sometimes three carpels.) In the wild it grows in open woodland on dry slopes. In cultivation the leaves can unfold very early in the year and are sometimes damaged by frost.

P. lactiflora
Distributed widely in East Asia including China, Japan, Korea and Siberia, *P. lactiflora* grows in open woodland or grassland where it flowers from May through to early July. Wild plants grow to around 1m tall and generally have 3-4 flowers on each stem. Flowers have 9-13 white or pink petals. They are the ancestors of a huge number of cultivars which are valued for their ability to produce side buds, increasing the number of flowers per plant and extending the flowering season.

P. mairei
This early-flowering species has deeply veined leaves and solitary pink to reddish single flowers. It is

Flower of
Paeonia mairei

Flower of
*Paeonia
mascula*

found in deciduous forests in China, and in cultivation will grow happily in semi-shade under trees or open shrubs. The name commemorates the French missionary, Edouard-Ernest Maire (1848-1932) who botanised in western China. The flower is rumoured to smell of nutmeg, but sadly not all plants do so.

P. mascula

The so-called male peony is widely distributed from northern Spain to Iraq, in broadleaved or coniferous forests, mostly on limestone. It was widely grown in monastery gardens for its medicinal properties and this is thought to be the origin of the naturalised population on Steep Holm Island in the Bristol Channel. Plants grow to around 80cm tall and have handsome leaves with broad leaflets that have rounded ends. The single flowers are usually a deep magenta-pink, and open early in the season. It is a robust, healthy plant that flowers well in light shade under trees.

P. obovata AGM

A widespread species found in China, Japan, Korea and eastern Russia, grow-ing in deciduous or coniferous forests. Plants vary from 30-70cm tall with stems bearing single flowers which may be white, pink or purplish-red. The white form is particularly desirable. In the garden it may be damaged by late frosts.

P. officinalis

A very variable species across its range from the Iberian Peninsula to the Balkans, P. officinalis was, like P. mascula, widely cultivated for its medicinal properties. It was known as the female peony on account of its foliage, which is finer, more 'ladylike', than that of P. mascula. The flowers are solitary and magenta-pink or red. A number of different forms, both singles and doubles, have been cultivated over the years. 'China Rose'

Leaves of *Paeonia officinalis*

is a clear, bright-pink single, especially effective when backlit by the sun. The well-known 'Rubra Plena' AGM may be a hybrid between *P. officinalis* and *P. peregrina*.

Paeonia officinalis 'China Rose'

P. peregrina (syn. *P. romanica*)
The red peony of Constantinople is found not just in Turkey but also in Albania, Bulgaria, Greece, Italy, Macedonia, Moldova, Romania and Serbia, growing in mixed forests or sometimes in grasslands. It has rich green foliage with toothed edges to the leaflets. The single flowers are a glossy red and are held in a cup shape. It is an excellent garden plant with very healthy foliage. The flowers have an irresistible attraction to bumblebees. Lateral roots may extend for some distance from the crown of the plant and can send up new shoots, giving rise to the development of a large open clump. Any fragments of root left when a plant is moved may re-grow to form a new plant.

Paeonia peregrina with bumblebee

P. tenuifolia

This is a very desirable species with many finely divided leaflets giving the plant a ferny appearance. It is variable, and can grow from 18-60 cm tall. Most plants have single deep-red flowers, but there is a double red, quite widely available in cultivation, as well as pink, white and double pink forms. Wild plants have been observed with white flares on red petals. *P. biebersteiniana*, *P. carthalinica* and *P. lithophila* have been described as independent species related to *P. tenuifolia* but Hong (2010) considers these forms to be within the natural variability of *P. tenuifolia*.

Flower and leaves of *Paeonia tenuifolia* 'Rosea'

'America' (Rudolph 1976)

A very dramatic, single red, hybrid raised by Nathan Rudolph of Illinois as a seedling from 'Burma Ruby'. The flowers are some 30% bigger than those of its parent and it has good stout stems. It was awarded a Gold Medal by the American Peony Society in 1992.

'Anemoniflora Rosea' AGM (unknown)

This cultivar of *P. officinalis* is a short-growing plant, to about 50cm, with sturdy stems and attractive glaucous leaves. It provides a bright splash of colour early in the peony season. The glossy petals are a rich cerise with a mass of yellow-edged purple-pink staminodes in the centre. It flowers well in dappled shade.

'Antwerpen' (pre-1928)

A cultivar of *P. lactiflora*, with very large flowers of Japanese-type, having pink guard petals, which curl back on themselves at the edges and a large centre of yellow stamens. The foliage usually retains its bronze colour well into the summer.

'Avant Garde' (Lemoine 1907)
Raised in France by Victor Lemoine
and his son Emile, who were
influential plant breeders, also famous
for their lilacs. 'Avant Garde' is from
a cross between *P. lactiflora* and *P.
daurica* subsp. *wittmanniana*. It is an
attractive plant, growing to around
75cm, with large, thick, healthy
leaves. It flowers early in the peony
season with beautiful single flowers to
15cm in diameter of a pale rose-pink.
The petals have a crinkled texture and

Paeonia 'Avant Garde'

surround a mass of golden stamens
and a plum-coloured heart. There are
usually three hairy carpels. Of the
same origin are 'Le Printemps', with
yellowish-cream flowers, and the
salmon-pink 'Mai Fleuri'.

'Bowl of Beauty' AGM (Hoogendoorn
1949)
A popular and widely available
Japanese type, raised in the
Netherlands. It has rose-pink guard
petals surrounding a mass of creamy
coloured staminodes. It is a reliable
garden plant and looks particularly
effective growing with blue and white
Campanula persicifolia.

'Buckeye Belle' (Mains 1956)
Deservedly a very popular plant,
'Buckeye Belle' is robust, disease
resistant and very beautiful. The semi-
double flowers are a glowing blood-
red colour and look spectacular in low
sunlight. A mature plant is usually
around 90cm tall, but the stout stems
do not generally need support.

'Candy Stripe' (Anderson 1981)
Introduced by Roger Anderson who is
better known for his Itoh hybrids, this
is a double *P. lactiflora* cultivar with
unusual flowers, striped white and
raspberry-red. It has long sturdy stems

Paeonia
'Buckeye Belle'

and makes a good cut flower with a light fragrance.

'Carnival' (Glasscock 1985)
Bred by Lyman Glasscock of Illinois and introduced by his daughter Elizabeth Falk, this is a very showy *P. lactiflora* cultivar with rich carmine-pink guard petals and a large central crown of pink and cream. It forms lots of side buds, giving it an extended flowering period. (There is also a tree peony with this name grown by Jane and Trevor Sutherland of New Zealand).

Paeonia lactiflora 'Carnival'

'Charm' (Franklin 1931)

A Japanese type *P. lactiflora* cultivar with dusky, deep mahogany-red guard petals surrounding a mass of yellow and red staminodes, this is valuable for its flowers late in the season. 'Red Charm' is a different plant, with vivid red, very large, double flowers.

'Chocolate Soldier' (Auten 1939)

Raised by Edward Auten of Illinois from a cross between *P. lactiflora* and *P. officinalis*, this is a vigorous plant with dark green foliage and deep brownish-red flowers. Whilst most of the flowers will be single, plants can sometimes throw fully double flowers amongst the singles.

Paeonia 'Claire de Lune'

'Claire de Lune' (White 1954)

Dr Earle White of Maryland made 500 crosses each season for eight years, using pollen of *P. mlokosewitschii* on the cultivar 'Monsieur Jules Elie'. Only one of the few resulting seedlings made it to maturity. 'Claire de Lune' has lovely creamy yellow flowers which usually open after its *P. mlokosewitschii* parent has finished flowering. There are several side buds on a stem, so plants flower for a longer period than do those of *P. mlokosewitschii*. The stems are straight and sturdy, so do not require staking, and it makes a good cut flower.

'Coral Charm' (Wissing 1964)

A vigorous plant, growing to around 1.2m, which usually needs staking. The large, semi-double flowers open a rich coral-pink and gradually change over several days through shades of apricot before fading to a creamy yellow. Mature flowers can be around 20cm in diameter. An established plant with open flowers in different shades always attracts attention. It is grown in huge numbers for the cut-flower trade in the Netherlands. The flowers are scented, but not especially pleasantly. If you move the plant, any fragments of root left in the ground can potentially re-grow, as with Oriental poppies.

Paeonia 'Coral Charm' recently opened (pink) and mature flower

'Crazy Daisy' (Klehm 1995)
A cultivar from *P. lactiflora* with bizarre semi-double flowers. The petals are puckered and ragged, mostly white, with lime-green mottling to the outer petals and random raspberry streaks.

'Dinner Plate' (Klehm 1968)
Another *P. lactiflora* cultivar, particularly recommended as a cut flower, this richly scented peony has long strong stems and very large frilly,

Paeonia 'Duchesse de Nemours'

deep pink flowers. The name is no exaggeration, as the flowers on mature plants can literally be the size of a dinner plate. The stems are strong but for garden flowers it is wise to stake the plant because it is quite tall (to 1.1m) and the flowers are heavy.

'Do Tell' (Auten 1946)
An unusual Japanese-type peony, with a ring of pale pink guard petals surrounding a mass of wavy staminodes in shades of pink and cream. It is a particularly floriferous cultivar and was awarded a Gold Medal by the American Peony Society in 2004. It has strong stems that do not usually require staking.

'Duchesse de Nemours' (Calot 1856) AGM
A popular, very free-flowering peony with double creamy-white flowers. It is an old French cultivar raised by Jacques Calot of Douai and named for Victoire, Duchesse de Nemours (1822-57) a portrait of whom is in the Royal Collection. The flowers have a lovely fragrance of roses with a hint of lemon. The peony is useful as a cut flower and is widely grown in the Netherlands for this purpose. It requires staking in a garden situation.

'Early Bird' (Saunders 1939)

A cross between *P. tenuifolia* and a form of *P. veitchii*, this is a lovely plant for the rock garden or front of border at just 45cm tall. It has very attractive foliage that is intermediate between those of its parents, and rich, glossy-red flowers very early in the peony season. It is very attractive to bumblebees.

'Early Windflower'/'Late Windflower' (Saunders 1939)

A P Saunders had a very systematic approach to peony breeding and used his huge collection of species to make numerous crosses. He used pollen of the Himalayan peony, *P. emodi*, on *P. veitchii* to produce 'Early Windflower', and *P. emodi* pollen on *P. beresowskii* to give 'Late Windflower'. (*P. veitchii* and *P. beresowskii* are now both considered to be forms of *P. anomala*).

Both forms of 'Windflower' look like their *P. emodi* parent, with tall stems bearing nodding, single white flowers. They have several side buds on each stem, giving a long flowering season. 'Late Windflower' opens about a week after the early form but unless you grow both forms alongside each other in the garden, they are difficult to tell apart, and indeed in the nursery trade they are much confused and may often be supplied under the name *P. emodi*. Whatever the name, they are excellent plants and will grow happily in sun or shade. They are easily propagated by division but do not often set seed.

A *Paeonia* 'Windflower' hybrid with *P. suffruticosa* 'Cardinal Vaughan' behind

'Edulis Superba' (Lemon 1824)
An old, but still worthwhile early-flowering cultivar from *P. lactiflora*, raised by Nicolas Lemon at his nursery near Paris. The rose-pink double has a row of large, slightly darker guard petals. The flowers have a pleasant sweet, rose fragrance. They last well as cut flowers but may require staking in the garden.

'Emperor of India' (Kelway 1901)
A striking, Japanese-form peony, from *P. lactiflora* that is late-flowering, with very large flowers having two rows of broad guard petals of a rich magenta-purple. The name refers to one of the titles given to King Edward VII on the death of Queen Victoria. The title was formally abandoned under George VI in 1948.

'Festiva Maxima' AGM (Miellez 1851)
One of the classic peony cultivars from *P. lactiflora* that should be in every collection, this fragrant peony was probably raised by the noted peony and rose breeder, Auguste Miellez of Esquermes-lès-Lille, France. It has large, double flowers, which open to the palest blush pink, then quickly fade to a creamy white. A few of the central petals are irregularly splashed with crimson. It has good strong growth.

'Flame' (Glasscock 1939)
An early-flowering hybrid peony from a cross between *P. peregrina* 'Sunbeam' and a *P. lactiflora*. It was raised by Lyman Glasscock of Illinois, who wanted to create a range of early-flowering cultivars for the Memorial Day cut-flower market. (Memorial Day is a federal holiday in the US, observed on the last Monday of May.) The good long stems make it ideal for cutting. The satin-textured petals are of a particularly vivid pink.

'Gay Paree' (Auten 1933)
This Japanese-form cultivar has bright pink guard petals surrounding a central mass of creamy white staminodes which are tinted pink in the centre, reminding some people of Blackpool rock. It is one of the extroverts of the peony world, with fragrant flowers. The stems are sturdy and do not normally need staking.

'Hei Hai Bo Tao' (China)
Sold as 'Evensong' by Kelways, this tall cultivar is notable for its dramatic purple-bronze foliage. The semi-double to double flowers are a deep mulberry-red and are good for

cutting. Some imports of this cultivar from China turn out to have green leaves so it may be worth trying to buy it in growth.

'Hit Parade' (Nicholls 1965)
A tall plant, with large rose-pink flowers of the Japanese form which can vary in appearance depending on the season and the maturity of the plant. It is from *P. lactiflora* and was introduced for Colonel Jesse C Nicholls by Gilbert Wild and Son of Missouri.

'Illini Warrior' (Glasscock 1955)
A tall plant, with very vivid, rich-red, single flowers. As with its semi-double sister plant 'Illini Belle', the stems are not very robust and may need staking. The name comes from the Illinois or Illiniwek people who gave their name to what is now Illinois.

'Inspecteur Lavergne' (Doriat 1924)
A large peony from *P. lactiflora*, with frilly, double flowers of a rich crimson. The central petals may be edged in silver. It was raised by the firm Doriat and Sons of Lapalisse in France who bought the business of Auguste Dessert. The flowers have long straight stems and a long vase life. They are scented, but not with the most pleasant of fragrances.

Paeonia lactiflora 'Inspecteur Lavergne'

'Jan van Leeuwen' (van Leeuwen 1928)

A very popular cultivar of the Japanese form raised from *P. lactiflora* in Sassenheim in the Netherlands. It has good disease-resistant foliage and strong stems, so does not usually need staking. The pure white guard petals enclose a centre of golden yellow staminodes. There is a light fragrance.

'Kansas' (Bigger 1940)

A strong-growing plant from *P. lactiflora*, with sturdy stems that support the large double flowers. It is a bright fuchsia-purple colour and does not usually fade in strong sunshine. The breeder, Myron Bigger of Kansas, introduced a number of distinctive peonies over a period of 40 years.

'Krinkled White' (Brand 1928)

Good strong stems support crinkled, pure white single flowers which can have a hint of pink on first opening. Raised in the United States from *P. lactiflora*, it is tolerant of both winter cold and summer heat. It is a reliable plant for a mixed border.

'Lady Alexandra Duff' AGM (Kelway 1902)

Named for the Princess Alexandra, 2nd Duchess of Fife (1891-1959), whose family name was Duff, this is a reliable and very beautiful peony. The first bud to open on each stem is generally a double flower, with the outer petals blush-pink and those in the centre white. Flowers from the side buds are more usually semi-doubles. The flowers hold their shape well as they mature and are valued for their sweet rose-scent. In 1913 Kelways were offering plants of this cultivar for £5 each when cultivars such as 'Queen Victoria' were priced at 6 shillings.

'Laura Dessert' AGM (Dessert 1913)

Raised by Auguste Dessert of Chenonceaux in France, this is a good plant with sturdy stems. The flowers have white guard petals surrounding a mass of fringed staminodes of a soft creamy lemon. There is a good, lemony scent. Cultivar 'Primevère' (Lemoine 1907) is similar.

'Lotus Queen' (Murawska 1947)

A L Murawska was an Illinois railway engineer who bred many irises and peonies and regularly opened his River Grove Gardens, where he had thousands of peonies blooming each June. 'Lotus Queen' is one of his best selections from *P. lactiflora*, with pure white guard petals that cup the golden-yellow stamens, producing many flowers on each stem. It is an excellent choice for the mixed border and should not need staking.

'Monsieur Jules Elie' AGM (Crousse 1888)

Felix Crousse of Nancy named several of his peony varieties after French painters; this one is named for Jules-Élie Delaunay (1828-1891). The peony has great popularity as a cut flower, although in the garden the stems sometimes need support. It is a late-flowering cultivar from *P. lactiflora*, and has very large, domed flowers of a light rose-pink.

'Mrs Franklin D Roosevelt' (Franklin 1932)

One of the best peonies for cut flowers, with highly scented, double, shell-pink flowers on strong stems, this is a particularly floriferous cultivar and one of the earlier *P. lactiflora* forms. It was named for Eleanor Roosevelt (1884-1962) by noted grower and breeder Alonzo Barry Franklin of Minneapolis. It is very highly rated by peony enthusiasts.

'Myrtle Gentry' (Brand 1925)

Known as one of the most fragrant peonies, 'Myrtle Gentry' is a *P. lactiflora* form with long-lasting, fully-double flowers in a soft pink. It was raised by Archie Brand of Minnesota, who took over the Brand Peony Farms from his father Oliver Brand. Myrtle Gentry was a local schoolteacher who took a job in the Brand Nursery office, later becoming a partner at the firm.

'Noemie Demay' (Calot 1867)

One of the essential classic French cultivars, this *P. lactiflora* form is very highly valued as a cut flower due to its rich fragrance. Individual flowers vary from Japanese to double in shape with layers of petals in shades of pale pink, cream and apricot.

'Qing Wen' (China)

Sold under the name 'Symphony' by Kelways, this *P. lactiflora* form is promoted as a lavender-pink peony but it is difficult to see any lavender shade; it is a deeper pink than 'Sarah Bernhardt'. The double, ruffled flowers are around 11cm in diameter and pleasantly fragrant.

'Rosea Plena' AGM (unknown)

A rose-pink double form of *P. officinalis* with a ring of broad guard petals. Growing to around 50-60cm tall, this is good for early-season cut flowers.

The flowers have a light fragrance but an unfortunate tendency to fade quickly in bright sunlight.

'Rubra Plena' AGM (unknown)
The most commonly grown peony and a regular sight in cottage gardens, surviving for many years with minimal care. It was said by Parkinson in 1629 to be 'frequent in everie Garden of note'. It is usually listed as a cultivar of *P. officinalis* but may be a hybrid between that species and *P. peregrina*; it certainly seems to display hybrid vigour. The fully double flowers of a rich, cardinal-red require support if they are not to flop, although they do look lovely hanging over the edge of a raised bed. There is also a double form of *P. tenuifolia* called 'Rubra Plena'.

'Salmon Dream' (Reath 1979)
Raised by David Reath of Michigan from a cross between 'Paula Fay' and 'Moonrise', this first bloomed in 1974. It has very beautiful salmon-pink flowers that are semi-double, opening quite flat but becoming more double in appearance on maturity. It is a good compact plant with strong stems, excellent in the garden or for cutting.

'Sarah Bernhardt' AGM (Lemoine 1906)
Named for the French stage and early film actress Sarah Bernhardt (1844-1923), this is a very popular and inexpensive cultivar, widely grown in the cut-flower trade. The massive double flowers to 20cm across are rose-pink, sometimes with crimson flecks, and lightly fragrant. It opens late in the season, and is not really a good garden plant, as without support the lax stems will flop.

'Scarlet O'Hara' (Glasscock 1956)
Bred by Glasscock and registered by his daughter Elizabeth Falk, this is a very vigorous peony, with tall strong stems and large, vivid-scarlet single flowers. The flowers usually look pinkish as they develop. It is a hybrid between *P. officinalis* and *P. lactiflora*. As you might expect, it is popular in the southern United States, where it is more tolerant of hot conditions than many peonies.

'Shirley Temple' (Smirnow pre-1948)
Raised by Louis Smirnow (1896-1989) of New York, who is best known for introducing the Itoh hybrids to commerce. Named after the famous child star, this cultivar is from a cross between 'Festiva Maxima' and 'Mme Edouard Doriat'. It has big double flowers of soft blush-pink with occasional red flecks, opening about

a week before 'Festiva Maxima'. It is highly valued in the cut-flower trade for the good strong stems, which do not need staking. The leaves sometimes colour well in autumn.

'Sorbet' (Klinkhamer 1987)
This plant was named and introduced into the Dutch nursery trade by Luc Klinkhamer, who saw it growing at a medicinal-plant farm in Daeyang Moolsan, South Korea, where peonies, mainly of *P lactiflora* forms, or old vigorous clones, are grown for their roots, which are used in medicine. It is a frilly, double peony, with petals in three layers: outermost pink guard petals, then a creamy coloured layer, and a topping of more pink. It has a pleasant, light fragrance, and lasts well as a cut flower.

Paeonia lactiflora
'Sorbet'

'Top Brass' (Klehm 1968)
A very dramatic peony, bred in the United States from *P. lactiflora*. It has layers of petals like an ice-cream sundae, with creamy-white guard petals supporting a mass of yellow petaloids, with pale pink petals as topping. It is extremely popular as a cut flower with a strong fragrance.

'White Cap' (Winchell 1956)
A very striking Japanese form with a strong contrast between the beetroot-red guard petals and central, creamy-white staminodes. It makes an excellent cut flower with a strong, pleasing fragrance, particularly when the flowers first open. Plants produce a long succession of flowers.

'White Wings' (Hoogendoorn 1949)
This simple, elegant peony from *P. lactiflora* has snow-white, single flowers quite late in the peony season. The flowers are large and generously produced. It is quite a robust cultivar, able to withstand bad weather, but may take a while to get established.

'Zuzu' (Krekler 1955)
A very pretty, semi-double *P. lactiflora* peony that opens blush-pink, maturing to pure white. Raised by William Krekler of Ohio, who sold his entire peony plantation to Charles Klehm and son in 1977, this cultivar has short, strong stems, and is good for cutting.

TREE PEONIES

P. delavayi AGM
A variable species, from 20cm to1.8m, found in western Sichuan, Tibet and Yunnan in China. It grows in dry woodland or on grassy slopes and can often spread by suckering to form a thicket of growth. There are usually two or three flowers on a shoot. Flowers generally hang on nodding stems, although in some forms they face outwards. They vary in size to around 8cm across and are sometimes very sweetly scented. The flowers can be yellow (previously known as *P. lutea*), red, maroon, orange or sometimes white. They are very attractive to bees and butterflies. The dwarf species *P. potaninii* falls within the natural variability of *P. delavayi*, although to the gardener's eye it looks distinctive because of the way it increases quickly by stolons.

P. ludlowii AGM
This very distinctive woody peony is one of the easiest to grow. It forms a

substantial shrub to 3.5m tall with wide-spreading branches. It has handsome, bright-green leaves that are broader than those of *P. delavayi* and very jagged in appearance. The flowers can be sweetly scented, and are larger than those of *P. delavayi* and of a bright, clear-yellow. There is usually only one carpel, compared with two to four in *P. delavayi*. The plant sets seed easily and numerous seedling plants may be found around mature specimens.

Paeonia ostii

P. ostii

A native of Anhui and Henan provinces, this species is widely cultivated in China for use in traditional medicine. It has been the subject of controversy in the west, with some commentators treating it as a *P. suffruticosa* cultivar, synonymous with the plant 'Feng Dan Bai' (**White Phoenix**). However, Hong (2010) considers it to be a distinct species. The pure white, or occasionally pinkish, flowers are open and flattish and have a rich-maroon sheath enclosing five carpels. It is a very beautiful and vigorous plant.

P. rockii

P. rockii probably excites more admiration than any other peony. It

is a large shrub, to 1.8m tall, with attractive divided leaves. The large flowers are white, or rarely red, with distinctive large purple blotches at the heart. The anthers and filaments are creamy-white, as is the sheath around

A *Paeonia rockii* type

the five, or occasionally six, hairy carpels. It was named for Joseph Rock who, in 1925, saw a cultivated plant in the garden of a Buddhist monastery in Gansu Province. He arranged for the collection of seed, which was sent to the Arnold Arboretum at Boston, Massachusetts.

P. rockii has been used by Chen Dezhong of Gansu in the development of a group of extremely beautiful plants known as Gansu Mudans. Despite the spectacular nature of their flowers, these are tough and adaptable plants that are easy to grow. *P. rockii* itself can sometimes be prone to *Botrytis*.

'Alice Harding' (Lemoine 1935) (syn. 'Kinko')

Raised by Lemoine in France from the cross *P. lutea* **x** 'Yaso-okina', a pure white suffruticosa-type. It was named for Alice Harding, whose New Jersey garden had a world-renowned collection of herbaceous and shrubby peonies. Her work, *The Book of the Peony*, published in 1917, did much to promote peonies. 'Alice Harding' is a compact shrub with flowers that are clear-yellow and double, but tend to be hidden by the foliage. They have a light, lemon scent. The plant

was listed by the Japanese Chugai Nursery in Yamamoto in their 1940-41 catalogue, and seems to have been renamed 'Kinko' in Japan. This cultivar was used by Toichi Itoh to produce the first intersectional hybrids. Somewhat confusingly, there are also two herbaceous peonies sharing the name.

'Ambrose Congreve' (Smithers 1994)

Named for Ambrose Congreve, who owned the Mount Congreve estate and famous gardens near Kimeaden, Ireland, this shrubby peony was raised by Sir Peter Smithers from seed of an open-pollinated *P. rockii* plant. The plant first bloomed in 1986. The flowers are large, to some 18cm in diameter, and can be single or semi-double. They are a light blush-pink with deeper rose-pink flares in the centres.

'Anne Rosse' (Rosse 1961)

Raised at Birr Castle in County Offaly, Ireland, this has bronze-streaked golden-yellow flowers. Anne Rosse, the daughter of Leonard Messels of Nymans in Sussex, married Michael, the sixth Earl of Rosse in 1935. They had a shared passion for gardening and honeymooned in China. This plant results from a cross made from a plant of *P. ludlowii*, which was collected by the Earl in the Tsangpo Gorge in Tibet, and *P. delavayi* collected by the couple on an expedition to Yu in 1937. It was awarded the Royal Horticultural Society Award of Merit in 1961.

'Black Panther' (Saunders 1948)
Semi-double, silky looking flowers around 18cm across are of a very dramatic deep wine-red colour. It is a rather better garden plant than the similarly coloured 'Black Pirate', whose flowers, like many other cultivars with *P. delavayi* blood, often hang down and get lost among the foliage.

'Cardinal Vaughan' (Japanese/ Kelways)
A spectacular shrubby plant from *P. suffruticosa*, with huge semi-double flowers, it probably originated in Japan and was given its English name by the firm Kelways in 1897 in honour of Herbert Alfred Vaughan (1832-1903), who is buried in Westminster Cathedral. The satin-textured petals are of a rich magenta-purple, rather than a true ecclesiastical purple, but are very eye-catching, whether in sun or shade. Plants can become somewhat leggy, and are better pruned while young to encourage a more compact, multi-stemmed form.

Paeonia suffruticosa 'Cardinal Vaughan'

'Chromatella' (Lemoine 1928) (syn. 'Kinshi')

Originating as a mutation from the plant 'Souvenir de Maxime Cornu', this is a readily available plant, often sold under its Japanese synonym 'Kinshi'. The heavy bright yellow flowers have petals touched with rose-pink. They tend to hang down amongst the leaves.

'Crinoline' (Rivière 2005)

The Rivière family have been growing peonies commercially in the south of France since 1849. Raised from open-pollinated seed of the UK form of *P. rockii*, this recent introduction has large semi-double to double flowers of a purplish-pink, with slight flares at the base. The leaves are dark green, flushed with bronze.

'Dojean' (Smithers 1988)

Raised by Sir Peter Smithers at his garden Vico Morcote in Switzerland and named for his wife, Lady Dojean. Plants are vigorous with attractive mid-green foliage. The flowers, to 20cm in diameter, are semi-double with frilly white petals showing red flares at the centre and a ring of yellow stamens around the red-sheathed carpels.

'Dou Lu' (China)

The name roughly translates as 'pea green', and the heavy double flowers of this shrubby and ancient cultivar from *P. suffruticosa*, look greenish on first opening, fading to white as they mature. The flowers have a few purple patches at the bases of the petals. It is a low-growing plant with quite weak stems.

'Er Qiao' (China)

An interesting chimera, with large double flowers that can be magenta-red, pale-pink, or pale-pink splashed and streaked with red, all on the same plant. Red flares at the base of the petals indicate that there is probably *P. rockii* in its ancestry. The name recalls the Qiao sisters of the late Han dynasty, who were famed beauties in what is present-day Qianshan County, Anhui.

'Gauguin' (Daphnis 1965)

Nassos Daphnis, a New York artist, worked with the plants of William Gratwick, producing many brightly-coloured, hybrid shrubby peonies. 'Gauguin' was the result of crossing *P. lutea* (the yellow form of *P. delavayi*) with 'Shintenchi', a semi-double, pink *suffruticosa*-type. It has large, single flowers of an unusual combination of yellow and red shades, with the exact colour varying from flower to flower even on the same plant and suggesting the bright colours of a Gauguin painting. The plants are usually healthy, with attractive bronze-tinged foliage.

'Hei Hua Kui' (China)

The name roughly translates as 'King of black flowers'. This is a low, spreading shrub, with flowers of a deep mulberry-red. The leaves can take on attractive red shades in the autumn.

'Hélène Martin' (Cayeux 1986)

Raised by Jean Cayeux of France, better known for his irises, and named for his wife, this plant originated from a cross between the plant then known as *P. lutea* var. *trolloides*, and 'Gessekai', a Japanese semi-double white *P. suffruticosa*, also sold as 'Kingdom of the Moon'. The very large flowers, to 25cm across, usually have two rows of petals. They are a soft creamy-pink, touched with red at the base, and may have greenish stripes on the inner petals.

'High Noon' (Saunders 1952)

A vigorous, well-branched shrub, growing 1.5 to 2m. Semi-double soft-yellow flowers, with red blotches in the centre, are produced in profusion over several weeks. A mature plant can have more than 50 blooms open at the same time. In the USA it is said to frequently re-bloom in the autumn, but in the UK it seems only to do this occasionally.

'Ice Storm' (Smithers 1989)

Raised from seed of Smithers' hybrid 'Lydia Foote', this has very simple pure white flowers to around 25cm in diameter, with golden stamens at the heart. The flowers sometimes produce white petaloids in the centre.

'L'Espérance' (Lemoine 1909) (syn. 'Kintei')

An early hybrid between *P. delavayi* var. *lutea* and a Japanese tree peony, this plant has lovely single yellow flowers with red flares at the centre.

'Lydia Foote' (Smithers 1992)

Raised by Smithers as a first-generation seedling from the UK form of *P. rockii*. It first bloomed in 1978 and was named for the Victorian actress Lydia Foote (1843-1892), whose real name was Lydia Alice Legg. The peony is a frilly, semi-double white with red flares in the centre of the petals. Mature plants tend to produce fuller flowers to around 23cm across.

Paeonia 'Lydia Foote'

'Nike' (Daphnis 1987)
Named for the winged Greek goddess
of victory, this is a free-flowering
vigorous plant that first bloomed in
1976. It has two rows of coral petals
that have red flares at their base.

'Mrs Shirley Fry' (Japan/renamed by
Kelways)
A mid-season peony from *P.
suffruticosa*, with beautiful single to
semi-double flowers of pure white.
The foliage often colours well in the
autumn.

'Shimanishiki' (Japan)
A fascinating plant that occurred as
a sport of the red-flowered 'Taiyo'
from *P. suffruticosa*. Each flower is an
individual with some petals being red,
some white and others striped.

'Souvenir de Maxime Cornu' (Henry
1907) (syn. 'Kinkaku')
Raised in France by Louis Henry,
and named in memory of the French
botanist and director of the Jardin des
Plantes in Paris, Marie Maxime Cornu
(1843-1901). The beautiful fragrant

flowers, about 16cm across, are a blend of gold and apricot shades, with the petals edged in carmine. They are fully double, and nodding, so until the plant is large enough to look up to, it may be preferable to cut the blooms and display them in a bowl.

'Vesuvian' (Saunders 1948)

A vigorous shrub, with frilly double purple/deep maroon flowers and jagged foliage that can colour well in the autumn. It is said to be one of the longest blooming of the hybrid tree peonies.

Paeonia 'Souvenir de Maxime Cornu'

'Yachiyo-tsubaki' (Japan 1910?) (syn.
Eternal Camellias)
This is a deservedly popular peony of
the *P. suffruticosa* type. The very large,
semi-double flowers, have lovely silky
petals of a soft shell-pink, forming
a beautiful contrast to the bronze-
coloured foliage.

'Yao Huang' (Chinese) (syn. 'Yao's
Family Yellow')
This is an ancient Chinese cultivar
that was much prized at a time when
most shrubby peonies had red, pink
or white flowers. It is mentioned in
the *Record of the Tree Peonies of Loyang*
by Ou-yang Hsin written in the year
1034. He wrote that it had originated
with the Yao family of Hoyang. The
flowers are soft-yellow when they
first open but quickly fade to cream.
They are usually very full doubles, but
plants will occasionally throw single
flowers with ragged petal edges. The
foliage has attractive purple tints.

ITOH HYBRIDS

'Bartzella' (Anderson 1986)
Raised by Roger Anderson of Fort
Atkinson, Wisconsin as the result
of crossing 'Golden Era', a single *P.
delavayi* var. *lutea* hybrid, with pollen
from the semi-double *P. lactiflora*,
'Minnie Shaylor', 'Bartzella' has lemon-

*Paeonia
suffruticosa
'Yachiyo-tsubaki'*

yellow, fully double flowers which are pleasantly scented. The carpels are creamy yellow. It is a rather taller, more upright plant than the similar 'Garden Treasure'. It created quite a stir in the late 1990s when divisions were being sold for $1,000 each.

'Callie's Memory' (Anderson 1999) A spreading plant that produces long, branched stems of flowers over a long season. The flowers are a peachy-yellow colour with maroon flares at the centre, and the petal edges are lightly touched with maroon. It first bloomed in 1990 and is named in memory of Anderson's pit-bull terrier, Callie.

'Canary Brilliant' (Anderson 1999) This forms very little woody top growth, with most of the annual shoots occurring from buds below ground. It forms a mound about 70cm high, and has attractive, deep-green, healthy foliage and shining, canary-yellow flowers of 10cm or more across. The flower colour can fade as the bloom matures. It really needs to be planted in full sun to encourage flowering.

'Cora Louise' (Anderson 1986) Named by Anderson in honour of his grandmother, this is a very special plant, with large, semi-double white flowers, blushed pink and showing dramatic deep-lavender flares at the base of the petals. Some flowers can have a somewhat shaggy outline. The flowers are beautifully displayed on good strong stems, and the foliage can show red tints.

'First Arrival' (Anderson 1986) Roger Anderson's first intersectional hybrid. This is a very showy plant with dramatic lavender-pink flowers held above the foliage. The flowers fade somewhat to a softer pink as they mature. The foliage can take on beautiful red tints in the autumn, which extends the period of interest.

'Garden Treasure' (Hollingsworth 1984) (syn. 'First Dutch Yellow') Raised by Don Hollingsworth of Maryville, Missouri, 'Garden Treasure' is very like an herbaceous peony in habit, forming a compact mound of mid-green leaves. The semi-double, deep-lemon flowers are produced over about four weeks. The heart and carpels are touched with rose-red. It sometimes forms stray petals in the centre of the flower. It was the first Itoh hybrid to be awarded the American Peony Society Gold Medal, in 1996.

Paeonia 'Garden Treasure'

'Hillary' (Anderson 1999)
Very large shaggy flowers, which can be semi-double or fully double. A deep watermelon colour in bud, the petals open in shades of rosy-red, fading to a creamy- yellow as the flower ages. It has a spicy fragrance.

'Julia Rose' (Anderson)
Cup-shaped, semi-double flowers in an intriguing blend of deep-pink and apricot, fading to yellow as the flower matures. Forms an impressive plant with generous quantities of flowers over several weeks, but can be more prone to fungal attack than some of the others of this class.

'Kopper Kettle' (Anderson 1999)
Produces semi-double flowers of a rich copper colour with deep reddish flares in the centre. The flowers have a spicy scent. It is a very beautiful variety, but sadly not as vigorous as many of the other Itoh hybrids and can be slow to flower. It is sometimes sold as 'Copper Kettle', but 'Kopper Kettle' is the spelling used by Roger Anderson in the original registration document and is therefore the accepted version.

'Lollipop' (Anderson 1999)
The flowers vary from semi-double to double in form and have a slight fragrance. They are a buttery-yellow,

irregularly splashed with rosy-red, giving them a very distinctive appearance.

'Morning Lilac' (Anderson 1999)
Despite the name, this does not have lilac-coloured flowers, as they are more fuchsia or magenta in colour. It is nevertheless a lovely variety, with very large frilly blooms on an attractively domed plant.

'Old Rose Dandy' (Laning 1993)
Dramatic single flowers of rosy-purple with large dark flares in the centre. As the flower matures, yellowish-buff tints develop. There is a good freesia-like scent. It forms a rounded bush with a profusion of blooms, but seems to be less vigorous under UK conditions and needs careful cultivation.

'Prairie Charm' (Hollingsworth 1992)
This peony results from a cross between the herbaceous cultivar 'Miss America' with pollen of the hybrid tree peony 'Alice Harding'. It is a very robust plant, forming a substantial bush and tolerating bad winters. The flowers are light-yellow and usually semi-double, with light-red flares in the centre, but occasionally fully double.

'Scarlet Heaven' (Anderson 1999)
Raised from a cross between a seedling of 'Martha W' and pollen from the deep-red *P. suffruticosa*, 'Thunderbolt'. Semi-double flowers of scarlet silk are held proud of the leaves. It has good healthy foliage.

'Unique' (Anderson 1999)
This plant resulted from a cross between *P. potaninii* (now considered to be a form of *P. delavayi*) as the pollen parent, on the light-pink herbaceous peony, 'Martha W'. It is a very vigorous plant, with deep-green, finely-cut leaves. The upright stems are an attractive shade of red. The flowers are single and of a very pure, vibrant red.

'Viking Full Moon' (Pehrson/Seidl 1989)
A form with single lemon-yellow flowers that have reddish flares. The colour is paler than that of 'Bartzella' and 'Garden Treasure'. The plant has a fairly upright habit but the large flowers can tend to hang downwards.

'White Emperor' (Seidl 1989)
A semi-double white flower with light-purple flares, this plant occurred as a sport of Itoh's 'Yellow Emperor' and was introduced by William J Seidl of Wisconsin.

'Yellow Dream' (Itoh 1974)

One of the four original Itoh seedlings, with 'Yellow Crown', 'Yellow Emperor' and 'Yellow Heaven', created from the successful cross of 'Alice Harding' with *P. lactiflora* 'Kakoden'. All four cultivars have semi-double, yellow flowers with red flares at the base of the petals, and have become somewhat confused in cultivation. They were registered with the American Peony Society in 1974 by the American grower Louis Smirnow. They are interesting garden plants, but not as showy as the modern American hybrids. 'Yellow Dream' has soft-lemon flowers with very pale flares at the base of some petals. The ring of green carpels in the centre is quite prominent. It has a light, unappealing scent.

Itoh hybrid 'Yellow Dream'

BEST-CHOICE LISTS

FOR SCENT
Described in the Directory of Peonies section:
'Duchesse de Nemours' AGM – Pond's cold cream
'Edulis Superba' – sweet rose
'Lady Alexandra Duff' AGM – sweet rose
'Laura Dessert' AGM – citrus
'Marie Crousse' – sweet, hints of spice
'Mrs Franklin D Roosevelt' – exquisite
'Myrtle Gentry' – rose

Others include:
'Kelway's Glorious' – strong rose
'Moon over Barrington' – spicy
'White Innocence' – musk and bubblegum

FOR CUTTING
Described:
'Coral Charm' – coral, semi-double
'Mrs Franklin D Roosevelt' – pink, double
'White Cap' – beetroot-red and white, Japanese

Others:
'Big Ben' – red, double
'Charlie's White' – white, double
'Chippewa' – red, double
'Felix Supreme' – red, double
'James Pillow' – pink, double
'Paul M Wild' – red, double
'Pink Dawn' – pink, single

FOR EXTENDING THE SEASON
Described:
'Emperor of India' – magenta-purple, Japanese
'Monsieur Jules Elie' AGM – rose-pink, double
'Myrtle Gentry' – soft-pink, double

Others:
'Beatrice Kelway' – deep pink, Japanese
'Fair Rosamond' – apricot-pink, Japanese
'Glory Hallelujah' – rose-red, double
'Lorna Doone' – rose-pink, double
'Mischief' – pink, single
'Silver Flare' – carmine, edged in silver, single
'Solange' – creamy apricot, double

FOR AUTUMN LEAF-COLOUR
(Autumn colour in peonies is very weather-dependent, being better with cold nights and sunny days.)
Described:
'Hei Hua Kui' – deep red, tree peony
'Mrs Shirley Fry' – white, tree peony
'Shirley Temple' – pink, double
'Vesuvian' – deep red, tree peony

Others:
'Charlie's White' – white, double
'Cherry Hill' – red, double
'Felix Crousse' AGM – red, double
'Le Jour' – white, single
'Peter Brand' – red, double
'Primevère' – cream, double

FURTHER INFORMATION

BIBLIOGRAPHY

Fearnley-Whittingstall, Jane 1999. *Peonies: The Imperial Flower.* Trafalgar Square. ISBN 0-297-82424-4.

Gunn, Spence 2005. New life for lilac, *The Plantsman*, 4,1 (March 2005) pp. 21-23.

Harding, Alice and Roy G Klehm (Ed.) 1993. *The Peony.* Batsford. ISBN 0-7134-7477-7.

Hong De-Yuan 2010. *Peonies of the World: Taxonomy and Phytogeography.* Royal Botanic Gardens, Kew. ISBN 978-1-84246-392-5.

Hong De-Yuan 2011. *Peonies of the World: Polymorphism and Diversity.* Royal Botanic Gardens , Kew. ISBN 978-1-84246-458-8.

McMillan Browse, Philip 2011. Plant ageing and its effect on stem cuttings. *The Plantsman*, 10,1 (March 2011) pp. 16-19.

Osti, Gian Lupo 1999. *The Book of Tree Peonies.* Umberto Allemandi. ISBN 88-422-0750-0.

Page, Martin 2005. *The Gardener's Peony: Herbaceous and Tree Peonies.* Timber Press. ISBN 0-88192-694-9.

Rogers, Allan 1995. *Peonies.* Timber Press. ISBN 0-88192-317-6.

WHERE TO SEE PEONIES

Abbey Dore Court, Nr Hereford HR2 0AD.
Tel: 01981 240419
www.abbeydorecourt.co.uk

Cambridge University Botanic Gardens, 1 Brookside, Cambridge CB2 1JE.
Tel: 01223 336265
www.botanic.cam.ac.uk/Botanic/Home.aspx

Hidcote Manor Garden, Hidcote Bartrim, near Chipping Campden, Gloucestershire GL55 6LR.
Tel: 01386 438333
www.nationaltrust.org.uk/main/w-vh/w-visits/w-findaplace/w-hidcote.htm

Highdown Gardens, Littlehampton Road, Worthing, West Sussex BN12 6PG.
Tel: 01903 501054
www.highdowngardens.co.uk

Penshurst Place, Penshurst, Tonbridge, Kent TN11 8DG.
Tel: 01892 870307
www.penshurstplace.com

The Royal Botanic Gardens, Kew, Richmond, Surrey TW9 3AB.
Tel: 020 8332 5655
www.kew.org

Spetchley Park Gardens, Spetchley, Worcestershire. WR5 1RS.

Tel: 01453 810303
www.spetchleygardens.co.uk

NATIONAL PLANT COLLECTIONS
Paeonia – **Hybrid Herbaceous**
Claire Austin Hardy Plants; White Hopton Farm, Wern Lane, Sarn, Newtown SY16 4EN. Tel: 01686 670342; email: enquiries@claireaustin-hardyplants.co.uk; www.claireaustin-hardyplants.co.uk. Opening times: 09.00-17.00 Mon-Sat, 10.00-16.00 Sun, all year round.

Paeonia – **pre-1900 and early post-1900** *lactiflora* **cvs.**
Mrs M Baber, Green Cottage, Watery Lane, Lydney, Gloucestershire GL15 6BS. Tel: 01594 841918. Opening times: check the NGS Yellow Book.

Paeonia lactiflora – **pre-1940s cvs**
Mr D Root, Kelways Ltd., Barrymore Farm, Langport, Somerset TA10 9EZ. Tel: 01458 250521; email: sales@kelways. co.uk; www.kelways.co.uk. Opening times: see website or phone for details.

Paeonia **spp.**
Mr & Mrs R J Mitchell, Kingscroft, Elie, Fife KY9 1BY. Tel: 01333 330642; email: kingscroft@ care4free.net. Opening times: by appt.

SUPPLIERS
Bennison Peonies, The Grange, East Firsby, Market Rasen, Lincs LN8 2DB. www.bennisonpeonies.co.uk

Binny Plants, West Lodge, Binny Estate, Ecclesmachen Road, Nr. Broxburn, West Lothian, Scotland EH52 6NL. www.binnyplants.co.uk

Claire Austin Hardy Plants; White Hopton Farm, Wern Lane, Sarn, Newtown SY16 4EN. www.claireaustin-hardyplants.co.uk

Kelways Ltd., Barrymore Farm, Langport, Somerset TA10 9EZ. www.kelways.co.uk

Phedar Nursery, 42 Bunkers Hill, Romiley, Stockport SK6 3DS. www.phedar.com

PEONY SOCIETIES
The American Peony Society
Claudia Schroer, American Peony Society, 713 White Oak Lane, Gladstone, MO 64116-4607 USA. www.americanpeonysociety.org

The Hardy Plant Society Peony Group
Membership Secretary – Kath Cary, Thorncar, Windmill Lane, Appleton, Warrington WA4 5JN. www.hardy-plant.org.uk/specialist/peony/ default.htm

The Peony Society
Membership Secretary - John Richey, 55 Franklin Court, Brook Road, Wormley, Godalming, Surrey GU8 5US. www.thepeonysociety.org

GLOSSARY

Adventitious – growth that occurs at an unexpected location, such as buds developing on a root.

Anther – the part of the stamen that produces pollen.

Cambium – the layer of plant cells just beneath the bark.

Carpel – one unit of the female part of the flower. Also called a follicle in peonies.

Crown – the basal portion of the plant where roots and stems or resting buds meet.

Endemic – native in one country or a specific geographical location.

Eyes – another name for the growth buds seen on the peony crown.

Fusiform – spindle shaped; broader in the middle than at the ends.

Glaucous – having a thin waxy layer which gives leaves a bluish appearance.

Intersectional – between two botanical sections, e.g. *Moutan* and *Paeonia*.

Involucre – a leafy bract beneath the flowers, can sometimes be confused with the sepals.

Loess – a sedimentary soil formed from accumulated wind-blown silt.

Stamen – The pollen-producing reproductive organ of a flower, typically consisting of a filament and an anther.

Staminode – a sterile stamen, which in peony cultivars can take on the form of a petal.

ACKNOWLEDGEMENTS

I extend grateful thanks to all those members of the HPS Peony Group who have shared their enthusiasm, knowledge, plants and friendship over many years. Your helpful suggestions and inspirational gardens/allotments have taught me so much. This booklet really has been a Peony Group joint effort.